PRESENT-DAY PROPHETS?

When Jeane Dixon was eight years old, she was told she possessed the gift of prophecy. In her mature years, she went on to predict several events—astonishingly, many of them came to pass.

When Edgar Cayce was about the same age, he experienced a vision. Later in life, he displayed remarkable powers, both of healing and of prophecy, which were believed to be of benefit to thousands of people the world over.

The question this book forcefully and logically answers is whether these two world-famous personalities are truly authentic prophets of God.

Dr. Bjornstad's careful reasoning and thorough research gives his reply—an illuminating and irrefutable answer to the questions in many thousands of people's minds. . . .

TWENTIETH CENTURY PROPHECY

PROPHECY

JEANE DIXON
EDGAR CAYCE

James Bjornstad

DIMENSION BOOKS
Bethany Fellowship, Inc.
Minneapolis, Minnesota

TWENTIETH CENTURY PROPHECY
Published by Pyramid Publications for
Bethany Fellowship, Inc.

Copyright © 1969 by Bethany Fellowship, Inc.

Paperback edition, November 1970
    Fourth printing, December 1972

Printed in the United States of America

DIMENSION BOOKS are published by
Bethany Fellowship, Inc.
6820 Auto Club Road, Minneapolis, Minnesota 55431, U.S.A.

FOREWORD

In this age of the atom and of advanced electronic technology when science appears to dominate virtually every area of human experience, it is strange to see a resurgence of interest on the part of odd segments of mankind in the subject of occultism.

In Europe, particularly England and Germany, Spiritism or attempts to communicate with departed spirits are greatly in the ascendency, paralleling a decided descendency in church attendance. In Germany cults have developed dedicated to the worship of Satan. Unhappily, that practice, once considered medieval, is now spreading to the modern levels of society.

In the United States, a renewed interest in astrology, spiritism and non-Christian cults in general recently caused *Time* magazine to devote an entire cover story to the subject of the new cult of astrology.

Side by side with such developments has come an interest in prophecy, extrasensory perception, parapsychology, clairvoyance and precognition. Departments in large universities (notably Duke University for one) have for some time been seriously studying these, not as passing fads, but as distinct scientifically demonstrable possibilities.

With the publication of Jesse Stearn's book *Edgar Cayce—The Sleeping Prophet*, great interest was kindled in a man who, while in a self-induced trance, both prophesied and dictated remarkable medical cures, a large majority of which have been validated to the satisfaction of almost any skeptic. The posthumous work of Cayce goes on in the Association for Research and Enlightenment with its headquarters in Virginia Beach, from which a veritable torrent of books and literature have poured forth extolling Cayce's capacities and gifts.

One need only turn on the television set to see "Maurice Woodruff Predicts," or read the daily newspapers featuring Jeane Dixon's predictions.

Can there be any doubt then to the necessity of such a book as this? Whether it is generally known or not, all such mystical intrusions into the domain of theology bear inevitably in one way or another upon historic Christianity and the Person, Nature and Work of Jesus Christ; and the Church must speak to these issues as they affect her.

James Bjornstad has thoroughly researched the Association for Research and Enlightenment, Jeane Dixon's prophecies and other assorted areas, and as much as is possible within the limited scope of a book this size given scholarly and intelligent appraisals of the data. He writes as an Evangelical Christian, from the viewpoint of orthodox Christianity. His research is sound and his conclusions challenging and provocative. This book will doubtless be used by many as a spiritual roadmap through the labyrinth of contemporary occultism particularly where Edgar Cayce is concerned, and sheds much light upon the errors so abundant within the structure of the entire Cayce theology and movement.

It is a real pleasure to commend this effort to the Christian public and to those interested in the study of pseudo-Christian movements in our time.

May it accomplish the author's purpose, the contrast of light with darkness and truth with error for the sake of human souls desperately in need of the Gospel of grace, particularly in an age when "men have exchanged the truth of God for a lie and have worshipped and served the creation more than the Creator who is blessed forever."

Walter R. Martin
Director
Christian Research Institute
Wayne, New Jersey
April, 1969

ACKNOWLEDGMENTS

I should like to acknowledge, with thanks, the generous permission of the Association For Research And Enlightenment in allowing me to quote from all their sources and readings, as well as the use of the photographs printed; the generous permission of *Christian Herald* and *Harper's* to quote from their sources; and the generous permission of the James L. Dixon Co. for the photograph of Jeane Dixon.

I should also like to acknowledge, with thanks, the help of the staff at the Christian Research Institute; Walter R. Martin for his help in the area of apologetics; Shildes R. V. Johnson for his help in writing the chapter on Atlantis; and Walter Bjorck, Jr. for the book reviews.

TABLE OF CONTENTS

Foreword

PART I

PART II

Part I

We have also a more sure word
of prophecy: whereunto ye do
well that ye take heed, as unto a
light that shineth in a dark place,
until the day dawn, and the day
star arise in your hearts.

II Peter 1:19

INTRODUCTION

Jeane Dixon has become one of the most powerful influences on the American national scene by virtue of what is claimed to be a prophetic gift. According to her biographer, Mrs. Ruth Montgomery, in her book *A Gift of Prophecy*, Jeane Dixon has filled the capacity as an unofficial advisor to Presidents, Prime Ministers, Congressmen and other dignitaries, in or visiting Washington, D.C. One perceives even more of her greatness in Jeane Dixon's latest book, *My Life and Prophecies*.

Her syndicated columns of predictions have been heralded in similar fashion to any Presidential announcement or address, and for many, her predictions are of greater import than any statement made by the President. Yet, her predictions, to at least some extent, are of great political import and certainly deal with the American political scene.

The Biblical prophets of old were also actively involved in the political situation of their times. This is attested to by the fact that it was the prophet Samuel who anointed Saul king. These prophets were also advisors to the various heads of State. When King Saul needed advice, he came to the prophet Samuel, at one point even after Samuel had died (I Samuel 28). King David had an advisor in the prophet Nathan.

When this aspect of the prophetic ministry is combined with the great accuracy of Jeane Dixon's prognostications which is claimed for her, some would say, as Jerome Ellison has stated it, that she "is probably about the nearest thing to an authentic but untypical Old-Testament-style prophet our generation of Americans is likely to see."

The late Dr. Daniel A. Poling was so correct in his review of the book *A Gift of Prophecy* when he stated: "This book is perhaps the most important volume that has appeared in the field of prophecy since the Biblical prophets." *My Life and Prophecies* by Jeane Dixon and Rene Noorbergen is of equal importance in this field.

They are important because if Jeane Dixon's gift of prophecy is the Scriptural gift of prophecy, and if God has raised her up to fulfill a mission to our nation as He had raised up the prophets of old, then Christians as well as the entire nation of America would do well to give her claims careful consideration. But, on the other hand, if God has not raised her up to fulfill a mission to our nation, and if she is not a true prophetess of God, then Christians must become aware of this fact lest America be deceived by someone coming in the name of the Lord, but not really being sent by God.

The question which we must seek an answer for is whether or not Jeane Dixon is an authentic prophetess of God in the true Biblical sense.

1. LIFE OF JEANE DIXON

JEANE DIXON has led one of the most interesting of lives. She was born Jeane Pinckert in Medford, a small lumbering village in Wisconsin, in the year 1918. Her mother and father, Emma Von Graffee and Frank Pinckert, were well-to-do Roman Catholic Germans who had come to America on their honeymoon. They liked America so much that Frank Pinckert sold all his interests in Germany and decided to live here in America.

By the age of 45, Frank Pinckert had amassed a comfortable fortune and retired from his business interests. He had been very much interested in and involved with the American Indians, not to mention also his great interest and fascination with nomadic gypsies. He was also a very close and intimate friend of Luther Burbank, the great horticulturist.

When Jeane Pinckert was very young, the Pinckert family moved to Santa Rosa, California. One day her parents received word that a gypsy woman had camped on the estate of Luther Burbank. Frank Pinckert told his wife to take Jeane, then eight years of age, to the gypsy. When Mrs. Pinckert and Jeane arrived, the gypsy woman was telling another woman her fortune by the use of cards.

When Jeane's turn came, the gypsy woman looked at her hands and declared she had never before seen lines like these. In her left hand she saw the Star of David with double lines leading from it.

In the right hand, another star on the Mount of Jupiter. She declared that Jeane Pinckert was blessed with the gift of prophecy and that she would foresee world-wide changes. She then warned Mrs. Pinckert to protect this child from people because she was gifted with this unusual sensitivity. This reading of the hands of Jeane Pinckert by the gypsy woman was later substantiated by a Hindu mystic, who saw the same stars and lines.

The gypsy woman went into her covered wagon, and returned with a crystal ball. Jeane was told that she could meditate upon this object and see great things. Jeane peered into the crystal ball and suddenly a picture formed before her. She saw waves of blue water and an island, the one from which the gypsy probably came. She saw the gypsy woman over a cooking pot, and sensed danger. She warned the gypsy woman to be careful with her cooking pot, lest she scald herself. The next time Mrs. Pinckert and Jeane returned, the gypsy woman's hands were bandaged. She had scalded herself with water from the cooking pot.

Jeane Pinckert also received an incomplete deck of cards from the gypsy woman, which were blessed for receiving vibrations.

Jeane used the crystal ball as a plaything, and thought that everyone could see the beautiful pictures which she saw in it. Her mother encouraged her to use and develop these gifts which were given to her by God.

Jeane Pinckert was one of seven children in the Pinckert family. From the earliest days, she was quite different from the other six. When she was just barely able to speak, she had toddled over to the door one day, and asked if she could play with a letter which was trimmed in black. No one paid much attention to it, until ten days later, when a letter trimmed in black arrived, announcing a death in the family.

Jeane also had a German nursemaid, Mother Koosey. When she would have visions as a small child, it was Mother Koosey who would interpret and explain to Jeane the meaning of her visions.

As Jeane grew up she learned more about her psychical powers and developed them as well as new channels to receive this information.

In addition to her great mystical abilities which she believed came from God, she was also gifted with a lovely mezzo-soprano voice, as well as considerable acting ability.

She made two appearances at the Hollywood Bowl. The first was when she was 21, she was chosen to play the supporting role of Mary Magdalene in *The Life of Christ*. Later, she was chosen to play the role of the lady-in-waiting in Shakespeare's *Midsummer Night's Dream*.

Jeane Pinckert had always had a crush on Jimmy Dixon, a son of a Methodist minister, and much older than Jeane. He was in the automobile business, and she had known him for many years. One day, her friends had invited her to accompany them to the Hollywood track. The first race was in progress, and her friends had asked her to place their bets for them on the second race. As she was rushing to the betting window, she crashed head-first into Jimmy Dixon. Jimmy Dixon, upon recovering, stated to his friend Bert Northrup, "That's the future Mrs. Dixon."

That evening, he called on the telephone to invite her out to dinner with him and his mother the following evening. A whirlwind courtship ensued, and within five weeks, they were married. Twice, during that period, however, she returned the engagement ring.

In order to marry James Dixon, who was a divorced man, it was necessary for the Roman Catholic Church to sanction their wedding by ecclesiastical dispensation. The wedding took place in San Diego, and they were united in marriage by a Roman Catholic Priest.

Following their marriage, Mr. Dixon continued in his automobile business, and Mrs. Dixon kept busy as a volunteer worker with bundles for Britain. It should be noted here that Jeane Dixon has always been interested in and worked for the cause of humanitarianism.

Then on December 7, 1941, Pearl Harbor was attacked. To be of help to America, the Dixons gave up their beautiful landscaped home and swimming pool in Los Angeles, California. Mr. Dixon volunteered his services to the Government. Mrs. Dixon volunteered her services in Home Hospitality Committees, while traveling with her husband, providing recreation and entertainment for servicemen and convalescents.

By the fall of 1944, several of Jeane Dixon's articles containing predictions found their way into the Washington Newspapers. Then in November of the same year, President Franklin D. Roosevelt invited Jeane Dixon to the Nation's Capital. That was her first visit to the White House. In 1952, Jeane Dixon's predictions became prominent in a syndicated column by Mrs. Ruth Montgomery.

The Dixons had moved to Washington where both of them could work in an extensive Real Estate business, which is still operative today.

In moving to Washington, they had a slight disagreement in the choice of houses while househunting. Mr. Dixon liked one house on Sheridan Circle in the heart of Embassy Row. However, Mrs. Dixon liked an older house on Nineteenth Street. Mr. Dixon thought the house outrageously priced, but Mrs. Dixon walked into her house and felt God putting His arms around her. Mrs. Dixon signed the papers and began the enormous task of redecorating and restoring the house.

At first Mr. Dixon was stubborn and refused to move into their new house; but about three weeks later, after seeing all of Jeane Dixon's work on the house, he was ready to move in.

The Dixon's have a happy and lovely marriage relationship. Every night, without fail, Mr. Dixon places a fresh sweetheart rose on her pillow. If he is out of town, he has a rose delivered daily.

Every evening, Jeane Dixon takes time out for self examination. She places her life and day squarely before God. Every morning, she begins by standing at her bedroom window, facing the east, and repeating the Twenty-Third Psalm. Then she attends Mass, which she has done every morning of her life.

Healthwise, Jeane Dixon eats almost no meat. Her diet is composed primarily of vegetables, fruits and juices. She does not drink or smoke.

Jeane Dixon has never accepted remuneration for her talent which she believes was bestowed upon her by God, for the special purpose of helping mankind. She believes that if she were to accept money for her services, her gift might be taken from her.

Jeane Dixon has always been interested in and involved in the humanitarian effort. She has volunteered for numerous activities, and has always been greatly interested in charitable works. She has helped to support a large number of poor white and Negro families. She has taken misfits, strangers and immigrants into her home, as well as given guidance and assistance to numberless teenagers who have gotten themselves into trouble, including unmarried girls who have become pregnant, runaways, etc. She is forever helping people of all types in every way possible, even to the extent of using her psychic abilities. She has found hidden talents and career potentials for many people, and thereby helped them to fulfil their role in society. She is currently actively engaged in all kinds of humanitarian efforts, but especially now in a children's work which she has founded.

Even today, she is constantly sought for advice by people from all walks of life, from the leaders of the world to the outcasts of society. She is an intimate friend of many dignitaries and a participant in numerous Washington Social affairs. Her predictions are widely discussed and printed, and in 1965 a book about her titled *A Gift of Prophecy* by Mrs. Ruth Montgomery was a best seller. Today it appears as a paperback. In 1969, a new book entitled *My Life and Prophecies*, by Jeane Dixon and Rene Noorbergen appeared on the market.

Jeane Dixon is a fascinating personality, and just as fascinating as her life story is her "bag of tricks"; the many channels and techniques by which Jeane Dixon receives her predictive information.

2. BAG OF TRICKS

EACH MORNING, Jeane Dixon asks God to reveal anything to her which would enlighten and make for a better mankind.[1] These revelations come to Jeane Dixon through a great variety of channels. When one examines these channels through which Jeane Dixon receives her predictive and prophetic information, one discovers a veritable occultist's complete "bag of tricks."

In her "bag of tricks" one discovers the employment of such channels as visions, crystal ball, astrology, numerology, dreams, cards, an inner voice, ESP, mental telepathy, and finger-touching, used in the reception of revelatory information. Indeed this is part of the fascination one finds in Jeane Dixon: the fact that her information is revealed through so many different channels.

Perhaps this story began when Jeane Dixon was eight years old. Her mother brought her to visit a gypsy woman who was camping on the Burbank's estate. The gypsy woman read Jeane's palm lines, and discovered the Star of David with double head lines leading from it. This was interpreted as the symbol of the gift of prophecy. The gypsy woman declared that Jeane Pinckert would become very famous, and would be able to foresee great world wide changes.[2]

The gypsy woman went into her wagon, and returned with a crystal ball, which she gave to Jeane.[3] It was later revealed that she had also given Jeane a deck of cards, which she blessed to carry good vibrations.⁴ This was the beginning of Jeane Dixon's "bag of tricks."

Later, she added certain other channels. When Jeane was in her teens, she had learned astrology from a Jesuit priest.⁵ Here she probably learned numerology, since the two appear intertwined.⁶ We also know that she had visions in her childhood,⁷ as well as her teen years.⁸ As life progresses, other channels are added until the list of channels is complete.

The first channel in her "bag of tricks" is that to which the greatest stress and significance is given: visions. The definition of a vision, according to Jeane Dixon, "is a revelation; a revelation is a will of God and cannot be changed."⁹ Jean Dixon herself declares that she communicates the vision or revelation of God exactly as it is revealed to her. She states "undistorted, as I see them, as He showed them to me. The will of humanity does not change the will of God."¹⁰

It is quite clear that visions are unchangeable, since they represent the will of God.¹¹ But in contrast to this is the crystal ball which also provides knowledge of coming events. These are subject to change because of changing human conditions.¹²

In the light of this contrast, it is of great significance and interest to note Jeane Dixon's preference to her crystal ball (subject to human changes) over a vision (unchangeable as God's will) in at least one instance.

In 1952, through the channel of a vision which was revealed to her while she was kneeling before the statue of the Virgin Mary in St. Matthew's Cathedral, Jeane Dixon foresaw the violent death which was to claim the life of the Democratic President elected in 1960.¹³ But in April of 1960,

Jeane Dixon, through the agency of her crystal ball, foresaw the election of Republican Richard Nixon as President in 1960.[14] To this very day, Jeane Dixon insists that Richard Nixon really won.[15] It is strange to note that in reality she is claiming her vision to be wrong, despite the facts that by her own definition a vision is unchangeable, not to mention the fact that Democrat John F. Kennedy was elected President in 1960 as the vision had revealed.

One of the real problems in examining the visions of which Jeane Dixon was the recipient, is the fact that she very rarely records the exact source of her predictive information in advance. Usually, one finds out that it was a vision only after the event has been fulfilled.

There are exceptions to this, especially as one reads chapter 19 of Mrs. Ruth Montgomery's book, *A Gift of Prophecy*. In this chapter she deals with four distinct visions given to Jeane Dixon which would provide great insight into the future of mankind. Certainly these four are recorded and interpreted for us, looking forward to fulfillment in the future.

A second channel used by Jeane Dixon is the crystal ball. This agency is by no means infallible, but as we noted previously, is subject to change because of changing human conditions. It is quite clear that the majority of her revelations come as a result of her perusal of the crystal ball.[16]

The crystal ball is the channel used basically in her readings to find answers for other people. This is also the channel whereby Jeane Dixon occasionally misinterprets the symbols presented.[17]

A third and fourth channel used by Jeane Dixon is astrology and numerology, which are used to establish "good days" for receiving prophetic information[18] as well as provide help in her search for information in certain sections of the crystal ball.[19]

A fifth channel used by Jeane Dixon is dreams, in which certain events are revealed to her. She dreamed one night that there was a fire in one of the houses. She called, and found out her dream was true.[20]

A sixth channel used by Jeane Dixon is a deck of cards, used particularly as a channel to receive the vibrations of a person, and not to tell fortunes by cards. In fact, the original deck of cards given her by the gypsy woman was not even a complete deck.[21]

A seventh channel used by Jeane Dixon is an inner voice which speaks to her revealing certain information.[22]

An eighth and ninth channel used by Jeane Dixon is that of ESP and mental telepathy. These we might group under her psychic abilities to receive predictive information. Ever since early childhood, her mother had encouraged Jeane Dixon to develop her "sixth sense."[23]

There are many predictions which she has made by way of her psychic powers. Through mental telepathy, she forecast a Nixon victory in 1960,[24] and picked up President Johnson's mental telepathy regarding a decision he later changed his mind about.[25] Of great interest here is her statement about the prediction of the assassination of Senator Robert Kennedy. She said, "My vibrations regarding the assassination of Senator Robert Kennedy did not come to me as a revelation. It was purely a psychic discovery obtained through mental telepathy."[26] Since her psychic abilities are considered to be given to her by God, they too must supply revelatory information from God.

Actually, in Mrs. Ruth Montgomery's book *A Gift of Prophecy*, Mrs. Montgomery herself infers throughout the book that Jeane Dixon is a psychic medium, a person extremely sensitive to psychic manifestation. In fact she likens Jeane to a spiritualist medium of the Civil War days, Nettie Colburn, who was an advisor to President Abraham Lincoln.[27]

A tenth channel used by Jeane Dixon is finger-touching, another channel by which to receive vibrations. By touching the fingers of President Franklin D. Roosevelt, his vibrations told her that he had about six months or less to live.[28] By touching a photograph of a girl's fiance, Jeane Dixon received vibrations which foretold a marriage that would fail.[29] Both of these predictions were proved true in the events which followed.

Thus we have the complete "bag of tricks" used by Jeane Dixon in receiving predictions and prophetic information. The entire "bag of tricks" is all connected with belief in the supernatural, since they are believed to have been bestowed by God. Each method or channel contained therein provides that which Jeane Dixon needs in her endeavor to obtain from God knowledge of the future, as well as assistance in the present affairs of life.

This has been true in the past concerning the magical aspects of Biblical prophecy regarding the Hebrews, as well as the magical aspects of the heathen nations surrounding them. It is quite clear in the Old Testament that the practice of magic by the heathen nations was not attributed to the God of the Hebrews, and that many of the magical practices of the heathen nations were later assimilated into the Hebrew religious scene.

Moses clearly pronounces the abomination of such magical practices: "Thou shalt not learn to do after the abominations of those nations. There shall not be found among you any one that maketh his son or his daughter to pass through the fire, or that useth divination, or an observer of times, or an enchanter, or a witch, or a charmer, or a consulter with familiar spirits, or a wizard, or a necromancer."[30] Why? "For all that do these things are an abomination unto the Lord."[31] These magical practices were an "abomination unto the Lord."

In 621 A.D. in the great religious Reformation led by King Josiah, we find this passage by Moses providing the basis for the cleansing and reformation of the Hebrews. "Moreover the workers with familiar spirits and the wizards, and the images, and the idols, and all the abominations that were spied in the land of Judah and in Jerusalem, did Josiah put away, *that he might perform the words of the law* which were written in the book that Hilkiah the Priest found in the house of the Lord."[32]

This same principle regarding the abomination of magical practices is true in the transformation of one's life when one accepts Jesus Christ as Lord and Savior. At Ephesus, "many that believed came, and confessed, and shewed their deeds. Many of them also which used curious (literally, magical) arts brought their books together, and burned them before all men."[33]

"Basically, the occultist's 'bag of tricks' has no place in Christianity. This is not to deny that God has communicated through some of these channels in Biblical history. One need only read Matthew 2 and note the use of dreams (Joseph) and astrology

(Star in the East). But, if one seeks to obtain from God knowledge of the future, as well as assistance in the present affairs of life, one should do one or both of the following points."

One should consult the Bible which is God's revelation to mankind. It contains all that is necessary for salvation and living the Christian life, as well as providing us with information about the future. This information about the future will assuredly come to pass as God has stated in His Holy Word.

One can approach God directly through Jesus Christ, and therefore has no need of techniques or channels from which to receive information. Remember well the words of Isaiah the Prophet: "And when they shall say unto you, Seek unto them that have familiar spirits, and unto wizards that peep, and that mutter: SHOULD NOT A PEOPLE SEEK UNTO THEIR GOD?"[34]

The Christian, then, has no need of various devices to find God's revelation. He has access to God through Jesus Christ, and he has access to God's Written Revelation, the Bible.

NOTES

[1] Montgomery, Ruth, *A Gift of Prophecy,* New York: Bantam Books: 1966, page 160
[2] *Ibid.,* pages 15-16
[3] *Ibid.,* page 17
[4] *Ibid.,* page 29
[5] *Ibid.*
[6] *Ibid.,* page 90
[7] *Ibid.,* page 23
[8] *Ibid.,* page 47
[9] *Newark Sunday News,* June 27, 1968, page A 1

[10] *The Christian Herald,* March 1966, page 42
[11] Montgomery, Ruth, *Op. Cit.,* page 164
[12] *Ibid.*
[13] *Ibid.,* page 6
[14] *Ibid.,* page 110
[15] *The Herald-News,* October 19, 1968, page 1
[16] Montgomery, Ruth, *Op. Cit.,* page 23
[17] *Ibid.,* page 24
[18] *Ibid.,* page 90
[19] *Ibid.,* page 29
[20] *Ibid.,* pages 77-78
[21] *Ibid.,* pages 28-29
[22] *Ibid.,* page 20
[23] *Ibid.,* page 18
[24] *The Herald-News,* October 19, 1968, page 1
[25] *Harper's,* June, 1967, page 37
[26] *Newark Sunday News,* June 23, 1968, page A 1
[27] Montgomery, Ruth, *Op. Cit.,* pages 39-45
[28] *Ibid.,* page 47
[29] *Ibid.,* page 80
[30] Deuteronomy 18:9-11
[31] Deuteronomy 18:12
[32] II Kings 23:24
[33] Acts 19:18-19
[34] Isaiah 8:19

3. TRUE PROPHECIES

As WE examine the prophetic accuracy of Jeane Dixon, one becomes enamoured with the numerous prognostications she has made which have been claimed to have been fulfilled in the events which followed. Of this fact there can be no doubt.

Her prophetic record of fulfillment, however, needs some analysis as to the format of her true prophecies. Some of her predictions have been so obviously vague and general, it is almost impossible to be wrong. Some of her predictions lend themselves to a host of various interpretations, so that almost any condition occurring with even the slightest resemblance to the prediction can be counted as its fulfillment. Some of her prophecies are mere extensions of certain developments already in progress, only dramatized for the public. Others were future projections based on past crises. But one must also admit that Jeane Dixon has made some startling prophecies which have been fulfilled. These cannot be passed off by rational explanation or lucky guess.

While we can document the public predictions of Jeane Dixon, there are numerous privately-rendered predictions which we cannot. It is the private predictions which are used by the followers of Jeane Dixon to give the greatest support to her accuracy.

In this chapter, we are merely going to present the various prophecies made by Jeane Dixon, for which fulfillment has been claimed.

Perhaps the greatest and most memorable prophecy Jeane Dixon has made was the assassination of President John F. Kennedy. This is the prophecy which brought Jeane Dixon to the national forefront as the Washington Seeress.

It was in 1952 on a misty, rainy day, Jeane Dixon had entered St. Matthew's Cathedral for her morning meditation. As she knelt before the statue of the Virgin Mary, she had a vision of the White House. The date 1960 appeared, and she saw a young blue-eyed Democratic President assassinated.[1]

Her prediction appeared in *Parade* magazine on May 13, 1956. From the time of this vision in 1952 until its fulfillment on November 22, 1963, Jeane Dixon consistently prophesied the future assassination of the Democratic President in 1960.

Of great interest in relation to the late President John F. Kennedy is a slogan written by Jeane Dixon, which appeared in the Army Journal of 1946. "It's not what your country can do for you; it's what you can do for your country."[2] In 1961, John F. Kennedy slightly modified this slogan for his own campaign: "Ask not what your country can do for you; but what you can do for your country."

There are also numerous other prophecies which have been fulfilled in history. In the middle of January, 1945, Jeane Dixon predicted that President Franklin D. Roosevelt would die within six months.[3] This prophecy was fulfilled on April 12, 1945, when President Roosevelt died of a cerebral hemorrhage.[4]

In 1946, Jeane Dixon foretold that China would soon be communist in the not too distant future. On September 21, 1949, her prediction proved true, when the communists proclaimed a People's Republic in Peiping.[5]

She further declared that a partition would occur in India within two years. The fulfillment of this took place on February 20, 1947.[6]

In the summer of 1947, Jeane Dixon predicted that Mahatma Gandhi would be assassinated within six months. Historically, Mahatma Gandhi was assassinated on January 3, 1948, thereby fulfilling this prediction.[7]

Jeane Dixon predicted, in January of 1948, the re-election of President Harry S. Truman. She also forecast that the rival nominees in this Presidential contest would be Thomas E. Dewey and Harry S. Truman. She was correct on both counts. Thomas E. Dewey and Harry S. Truman were the nominees, and in November, 1948, Truman was re-elected President of the United States.[8]

In June, 1953, Jeane Dixon predicted that a Chief Justice would die within a few months. In September, 1953, Chief Justice Fred Vinson died, thus fulfilling this prophecy.[9]

She also predicted in 1953 that the AFL and CIO would merge in two years. This prophecy was validated on December 5, 1955, with the merger of the two unions.

One of the most fascinating incidences occurred also in May of 1953, when Jeane Dixon had met Bob Hope backstage. Bob Hope stated that he had been playing golf with President Eisenhower that afternoon, and challenged Jeane Dixon to tell him his score, if she was really as good as he had heard. She did, and Bob Hope had to cut the tape. If it went over the air, how would he explain the President's score, much less the fact that he had not revealed it?[10] Bob Hope had defeated President Eisenhower, 92 to 96.

At the Kentucky Derby in 1953, Jeane Dixon was confused over the fact that she could not see previously undefeated Native Dancer winning, but neither could she see him losing. It was explained to her that a horse need not come in first to be in the money. He could place or show. She decided that Native Dancer would come in second, and that was exactly what happened.[11]

It is claimed that Jeane Dixon foresaw several heart attacks for President Dwight Eisenhower in the year of 1955. All of these attacks are claimed to have come to pass as she had predicted. Because of these attacks, President Eisenhower was not sure that he would run for re-election in November of 1956. However, Jeane Dixon foresaw different.

In December, 1955, Jeane Dixon predicted the re-election of President Eisenhower which was fulfilled in November, 1956.[12] In an article in *The New York Daily News*, on December 31, 1955, it was stated that Jeane Dixon's "stars have already decreed that Dwight D. Eisenhower will be re-elected."[13] In that very election, Jeane Dixon predicted that Senator Estes Kefauver would be nominated as the Democratic nominee for the Vice-Presidency, which was fulfilled.[14]

Late in the year 1956, Jeane Dixon predicted the death of Jawaharlal Nehru which would occur in seven years. She also predicted the fact that the name of the man who would succeed him would begin with an S. On May, 1964, Jawaharlal Nehru died, and his successor's name was Shastri. Thus, Jeane Dixon's prediction was right on both counts.[15]

On December 28, 1958, Jeane Dixon stated that

the Secretary of State John Foster Dulles would die by the middle of the following year. Its fulfillment took place on May 24, 1959, with the death of John Foster Dulles.[15]

In the middle of September, 1961, Jeane Dixon foresaw the plane crash of Dag Hammarskjöld in the very near future. On November 18, 1964, this prediction was literally fulfilled in a plane crash involving Dag Hammarskjöld.[16]

In her column in 1962, Jeane Dixon predicted that Religion would play an important role in that year; a role greater than that which the public was now thinking. Fulfillment is claimed for this prediction in the decision by the Supreme Court, on June 25, 1962, to ban prayer in the public schools.

Late in the year 1962, Jeane Dixon predicted that Sir Winston Churchill would die by the end of 1964. In December 1964, Sir Winston Churchill passed away,[17] validating another of Jeane Dixon's prophecies.

On Friday, June 19, 1964, Jeane Dixon predicted a plane crash for Senator Edward Kennedy in the very near future. The next day, the crash took place as Jeane Dixon predicted.[18]

In her column in *The Herald-News*, January 27, 1968, Jeane Dixon wrote that there was a "dark cloud around Senator Kennedy with strings leading to his background, which I interpret as a tragic event in which he was an unwilling participant."[19] While this prophecy is very vague as to exactly what the tragic event would be, it is claimed that Jeane Dixon specifically told restaurateur James Matthews, back in January in Miami, Florida, that Senator Robert Kennedy would suffer the same fate as his brother John F. Kennedy. She said it would occur in California in June.[21] This prophecy was fulfilled in June, 1968 in California with the assassination of Senator Robert Kennedy.

Jeane Dixon predicted in her column in *The Herald-News*, October 19, 1968, that "Richard Nixon will be our next President."[21] On November 5, 1968, Richard Nixon was elected to the Presidency of the United States of America.

The above fulfillment of Nixon's election probably follows Jeane Dixon's great statement of 1962. After Nixon was defeated in California, Jeane Dixon told a news press conference that it would be his last defeat. She predicted that the future held a most important role for Richard Nixon in politics and for the United States.[22] This statement is claimed to be fulfilled in the election of Richard Nixon as President, despite its vagueness.

Again in the *Newark Sunday News*, June 23, 1968, Jeane Dixon predicted "steam roller" tactics on the part of some to get Senator Edward Kennedy on the Democratic ticket. She warned that if he did not run, and if he left things to God's time, he could prolong his life.[23] Senator Kennedy did not run and is still alive; providing somewhat of a fulfillment to the prophecy.

Regarding the U.S. submarine Scorpion, Jeane Dixon states in her column in the *Newark Sunday News*, June 23, 1968, "I saw the Scorpion. It had a long glowing tunnel behind it. I saw a deadly form rise up from the shallow ocean floor. It found the tunnel and turned into it, following in the atomic submarine's wake. It caught the submarine's rine with disastrous results."[24]

She further goes on to point out that there was another submarine, not ours, which "confused the search and gave false radio broadcasts."[25] While we do not have many of the details of this catastrophe, these statements of prophecy regarding the Scorpion are claimed as being fulfilled.[26] So far, only one portion has been conceived of as true; and that has to do with the false radio broadcasts which did lead our search astray.

It is also claimed that Jeane Dixon had predicted the death of Marilyn Monroe by suicide some nine months before it occurred.[27] In 1964 it is claimed that she predicted the Alaskan earthquake one month before it occurred.[28] It is further claimed that she foresaw the blackout which darkened the greater portion of the New England Coast, including New York in 1965.[29]

In January, 1968, Jeane Dixon stated in her column in the *Newark Sunday News*, June 23, 1968, that "she expected that boys will begin to look more like girls, and the men's fashion fad of beads, necklaces and even handbags was not long coming thereafter."[30] Needless to say, this prophecy is currently being fulfilled.

One must take notice, too, in presenting Jeane Dixon's prophecies, of her many personal prophecies, involving herself and her family. When she was sixteen, she predicted that when her sister Evelyn reached her sixteenth birthday, she would ask her father for a plane as a birthday present. This came to pass exactly as she said it would.[31]

Once, while in New York, she perceived that her mother had just passed away in California. She called, and her perception was true.[32] Then two years later while in Washington, she perceived that her father had just died also in California. Once again, her perception was true.[33]

In her latest book, *My Life And Prophecies*, Jeane Dixon presents several new fulfilled prophecies. She claims that as early as 1960 she foresaw that Martin Luther King, Jr. would be assassinated in 1968. In 1968 she predicted that he would be shot in the neck.[34] The assassination took place as predicted on April 4, 1968.

Jeane Dixon does not believe that James Earl Ray was the assassin. She believes the assassin to be a young male (late 20's, early 30's), with blonde hair, medium build and height. He is a Communist.[35]

On September 13, 1967, Jeane Dixon foresaw the death of Robert F. Kennedy. Later she predicted that he would meet the same fate as his brother, the late John F. Kennedy. She also predicted on March 28, 1968, that he would be shot while in California.[36] This came to pass on June 5, 1968.

In 1968 Jeane Dixon also predicted that the U.S. would soon have some serious trouble with North Korea. The USS Pueblo was captured a few days later.[37]

There can be no doubt but that a good number of the prophecies and predictions of Jeane Dixon have been borne out by events. Those which have been presented in this chapter do not exhaust the possible number of fulfilled prophecies, but illustrate the vast variety of fulfilled prophecies.

So far, we have focussed on the predictions and fulfilled prophecies of Jeane Dixon. But of equal importance in our study is the subject of the numerous false prophecies of Jeane Dixon, those which were never fulfilled as stated.

NOTES

1. Montgomery, Ruth, *A Gift of Prophecy*, New York: Bantam Books: 1966, page 6
2. *Ibid.*, pages 36-37
3. *Ibid.*, page 48
4. *Ibid.*, page 51
5. *Ibid.*, pages 52-53
6. *Ibid.*, pages 53-54
7. *Ibid.*, page 76
8. *Ibid.*, page 87
9. *Ibid.*, page 83
10. *Ibid.*, page 92
11. *Ibid.*, page 96
12. *Ibid.*, page 103
13. *New York Daily News*, December 31, 1955
14. Montgomery, Ruth, *Op. Cit.*, pages 102-103
15. *Ibid.*, page 30
16. *Ibid.*, page 83
17. *Ibid.*, page 101
18. *Ibid.*, page 13
19. *The Herald-News*, January 27, 1968, page 7
20. *Newark Sunday News*, June 23, 1968, page A 1
21. *The Herald-News*, October 19, 1968, page 1
22. *Ibid.*, page 1
23. *Newark Sunday News*, June 23, 1968, page A 1
24. *Ibid.*, page A 1
25. *Ibid.*, page A 1
26. *Ibid.*, page A 1
27. Montgomery, Ruth, *Op. Cit.*, page 81
28. *The Christian Herald*, March, 1966, page 41
29. Montgomery, Ruth, *Op. Cit.*, page 196
30. *Newark Sunday News*, June 23, 1968, page A 1
31. Montgomery, Ruth, *Op. Cit.*, page 21
32. *Ibid.*, page 58
33. *Ibid.*, page 59
34. Dixon, Jeane, and Noorbergen, Rene, *My Life And Prophecies*, New York: William Morrow and Company, Inc.: 1969, pages 109-121
35. *Ibid.*
36. *Ibid.*, pages 122-133
37. *Ibid.*, page 126

4. FALSE PROPHECIES

WHEN ONE first comes in contact with the prophecies and predictions of the famous Washington seeress Jeane Dixon, one is overwhelmingly impressed with the great accuracy which is presented to the general public regarding her prophetic record. As one examines the claims that have been made regarding her prophetic accuracy, one becomes aware of numerous prophecies and predictions made by Jeane Dixon which were never fulfilled.

It is not possible to know the exact number of errors she has made, primarily because no one has ever recorded all of her prophecies. Many of her prophecies were communicated orally, in private conversation with many different people, and some of these are generally impossible to prove either true or false, unless they were recorded somewhere on tape, in writing, etc. Generally speaking, the prophecies and predictions of Jeane Dixon can be traced back with accuracy as far as 1952, the year Mrs. Ruth Montgomery began writing her famous column on Jeane Dixon. Therefore one must examine the available records, and in so doing, one discovers numerous and obvious errors which have been proven by history itself to be "false prophecies."

In her column in *The Herald-News*, January 27, 1968, Jeane Dixon predicted that the Democratic nomination for the Presidency of that year would go to President Lyndon B. Johnson.[1] This prophecy was never fulfilled. Historically we know that at the Democratic National Convention in Chicago, Illinois, the Democratic nomination for the Presidency of the United States of America went to Hubert H. Humphrey. In fact in an earlier address to the nation, President Lyndon B. Johnson stated that he would not seek the nomination.

Jeane Dixon further predicted in this column, that "Mrs. Jacqueline Kennedy is not now thinking of marriage. She will marry only when time dims the memory of her late husband's assassination and the death of infant Patrick Bouvier Kennedy. Only at the very end of 1968 may she seriously consider marriage."[2] Again in her column in *The Herald-News*, October 19, 1968 the day before the wedding of Jacqueline Kennedy and Aristotle Onassis; even after the mass media had broadcasted news of this wedding), Jeane Dixon still stood on her New Year's prediction, seeing no marriage for Jacqueline Kennedy.[3] The next day proved fatal to the predictions of Jeane Dixon, for on October 20, 1968, Jacqueline Kennedy and Aristotle Onassis were united in marriage. It should be noted here that on October 19, 1968, while *The Herald-News* carried Jeane Dixon's statement backing her original prediction on January 27, 1968, it also printed a small bordered news item in the middle of Jeane Dixon's column, titled "Bad Day For A Seer." It stated: "Her negative vibrations regarding marriage centered on Lord Harlech." "Please delete reference in predictions to Mrs. Kennedy."[4]

When one reads Mrs. Ruth Montgomery's book on Jeane Dixon, titled *A Gift of Prophecy*, one finds even Mrs. Montgomery revealing the fact that Jeane Dixon has erred in some of her prophecies. She points out that Jeane Dixon predicted that Red China would plunge into war over Quemoy and Matsu in October, 1958.[5] Historically, this war never took place.

She further pointed out that Jeane Dixon wrongly predicted that Walter Reuther would actively seek the Presidency of the United States of America in 1964.[6] He was to receive the Democratic nomination and Richard Nixon was to oppose him as the Republican nominee.[7] Walter Reuther did not actively seek the Presidency in 1964, much less receive the Democratic nomination. Furthermore, Richard Nixon did not receive the Republican nomination either.

There is also an interesting contradiction in the predictions found in Mrs. Montgomery's book *A Gift of Prophecy*. She points out that Jeane Dixon predicted in 1952 that a young, blue-eyed Democrat would be elected to the Presidency of the United States of America in 1960.[8] But in August, 1960, Jeane Dixon seems to have changed her mind. Mrs. Montgomery points out that Jeane Dixon predicted a Nixon victory, a Republican President.[9] How then does Mrs. Dixon solve this apparent contradiction? She believes that Richard Nixon really won the election, but that the Presidency was stolen from him by certain dishonest vote counters. This is best expressed by Jeane Dixon herself in her column in *The Herald-News*, October 19, 1968. "During the 1960 election I saw Richard Nixon as the winner; I stated this in public and have never retracted this statement. This telepathy forecast was shown as a Nixon victory, taken away from him by a handful of men in the midwest. However, destiny cannot be denied."[10] Jeane Dixon's solution is basically the claim that Richard Nixon really won the Presidency, but

John F. Kennedy really got the Presidency. Thus, in a sense, both won.

In the *New York Daily News*, January 1, 1953, Jeane Dixon predicted that President Dwight Eisenhower would appoint General Douglas MacArthur to a very important post in his administration; probably to the post of an ambassadorship.[11] However, the record of history reveals no such appointment as ever having been made; in fact, Douglas MacArthur remained the chairman of the board of the Remington Rand Corporation until his death on April 5, 1964.

Jeane Dixon further stated in this column that "the astrological numbers of Generals Al Wedemeyer and Patrick J. Hurley are clearly intertwined. They should combine forces and solve the China problem."[12] These two men never "combined forces," nor solved "the China problem."

She also predicted that "one of Russia's allies" would "turn against her after the Soviet armies have pushed through Iran and into Palestine."[13] Jeane Dixon further predicted "that Russia will move into Iran in the fall of 1953. The bear will not move on to Palestine until 1957."[14] There is no possible way of interpreting the above prophecies to bring about their fulfillment. Historically, none of these events occurred as predicted.

At one point in her prophetic ministry, Jeane Dixon predicted that World War III would break out in 1958.[15] Needless to say, this prophecy never came to pass.

She also predicted that Red China would be admitted to the United Nations in 1959.[16] It is a clear fact of history that Red China was not admitted to the United Nations in 1959.

She further predicted that the Conservative

party of Great Britain would win in the election of 1964.[17] Again, history declares that this prediction was never fulfilled, for the Conservative Party of Great Britain was defeated in the elections of 1964.

On October 23, 1954, according to Mrs. Ruth Montgomery, Jeane Dixon insisted that by the year 1964, Russia and China would be ruled by a swarthy-skinned man who was part-oriental.[18] This never came to pass.

Jeane Dixon was asked on May 7, 1966, at the Hancock Auditorium of the University of Southern California how long the current war in Vietnam would last. Her answer was that this war would end in ninety days, but not on our terms.[19] Needless to say, this is another prophecy which was never fulfilled.

Even before the above incident occurred, Jeane Dixon stated on January 2, 1966, that peace negotiations concerning Vietnam would begin early that year.[20] One fact is certain; peace efforts continued through 1966 into 1967. But, there was no real negotiation taking place. In fact, at a press conference in February 1967, President Lyndon B. Johnson clearly stated that no real negotiation had taken place with Hanoi. Hanoi had not responded to our peace efforts. It is certainly clear, then, that this is another prophecy made by Jeane Dixon, which has no fulfillment in history as stated.

While studying her crystal ball one day in 1956, Jeane Dixon saw something which revealed to her that a new position in our Government was about to be created. This position was to be between that of the President and that of the Vice President. It would be greater than the latter office, and lesser than the former. This she interpreted as the revelation of a new position, that of an "assistant President."

In her crystal ball, she saw Dewey and Senator William Knowland vying for this new position. Dewey was to become the new assistant President and Senator Knowland was to become more prominent.[21] However, the new executive position of assistant President was never created, nor did Dewey ever become the first assistant President. The prominence of Senator Knowland was never fulfilled either, and he later took over the administration of his family newspaper, the *Oakland Tribune*.

One day, in the summer of 1966, Jeane Dixon was asked a question regarding Premier Fidel Castro of Cuba. According to her vibrations, she stated that Castro was either in China or he was dead.[22] Neither of these predictions proved true: Fidel Castro was not dead, and because of his country's hostility toward Red China, it was extremely unlikely that he was there at that time.

Furthermore, Jeane Dixon also stated in 1966, that our relationship with the French and particularly with French President Charles de Gaulle would improve in the very near future as a direct result of President Lyndon Johnson's appointment of a new ambassador to France.[23] This appointment was never made, and as a result our relationship was never greatly improved either.

Later, Jeane Dixon admitted that President Johnson had really intended to make this appointment; that she had merely "picked up his mental telepathy but he changed his mind."[24] In either case, her prediction did not see its fulfillment.

In 1967, Jeane Dixon was asked a question about the budding romance between Lynda Bird Johnson and George Hamilton. She replied: "He can bring more spirituality into the President's home than anyone I know. They would be lucky to have him."[25] But, this romance soon disappeared, and the Johnsons soon received a son-in-law, but it was not George Hamilton.

In her latest book, *My Life And Prophecies*, Jeane Dixon predicted a new vocation for Bishop James Pike.[26] This never was fulfilled as Bishop Pike died in the deserts of Israel even prior to the publication of her book.

Jeane Dixon also predicted that Russia would be the first to land a man on the moon.[27] The historical "Moon Walk" in 1969 has proven this prophecy to be false. The United States was first.

The aforementioned prophecies and predictions which have never been fulfilled as stated do not exhaust the subject of Jeane Dixon's "false prophecies." They are merely illustrative of the fact that while Jeane Dixon is indeed responsible for many great prophecies which have come to pass, she is also responsible for numerous "false prophecies." It is these "false prophecies" which will prove very important in our consideration of the all important question of whether or not Jeane Dixon is a true prophetess of God.

NOTES

[1] *The Herald-News,* January 27, 1968, page 7
[2] *Ibid.*
[3] *The Herald-News,* October 19, 1968, page 1
[4] *Ibid.*
[5] Montgomery, Ruth, *A Gift of Prophecy,* New York: Bantam Books: 1966, page X
[6] *Ibid.*
[7] *Harper's,* June 1967, page 38

[8] Montgomery, Ruth, *Op. Cit.,* page 109

[9] *Ibid.,* page 110

[10] *The Herald-News,* October 19, 1968, page 1

[11] *New York Daily News,* January 1, 1953

[12] *Ibid.*

[13] *Ibid.*

[14] *Ibid.*

[15] *Harper's,* June 1967, page 37

[16] *Ibid.*

[17] *Ibid.,* page 38

[18] Ebon, Martin, *Prophecy In Our Time,* New York: The New American Library: 1968, page 195

[19] *Ibid.,* pages 192-3, cf also the report of this session by Mrs. Michael Barton in the June-July, 1966 issue of the *Cosmic Star*

[20] *Ibid.,* page 193

[21] *Ibid.,* pages 195-6

[22] Ibid., page 196

[23] *Harper's,* June 1967, page 37

[24] *Ibid.*

[25] *Ibid.,* page 38

[26] Dixon, Jeane, and Noorbergen, Rene, *My Life And Prophecies,* page 155

[27] Seligson, Marcia: "Dixonmania," *The New York Times Book Review,* October 19, 1969, page 22

5. THE FUTURE WORLD LEADER

SHORTLY BEFORE 7 a.m. (EST), February 5, 1962, a child was born of humble peasant origin in the Middle East who will one day be the future World Leader. The great force of this man would be felt and understood in the early 1980's. His power would continue to grow until 1999, when we would have a world without war: a time of "peace on earth to all men of good will."'

This revelation or vision is really a mosaic of four distinct visions which Jeane Dixon has had in recent years. This mosaic of the four visions is believed by Jeane Dixon to be of enormous significance for all mankind.'

This particular series of visions began on July 14, 1952. It was about midnight as Jeane Dixon lay on her bed, drowsy but not really asleep. Suddenly she felt something moving against the mattress on the portion to the left side of her head. She rolled over on her left side, and was then facing east.

She noticed the body of a snake, approximately the thickness of a garden hose, there on the bed. Its body slid down the side of the bed, and at the bottom by the feet it raised up the corner of the mattress. Its head nudged her ankles and gradually wrapped itself around her legs and hips, making its way slowly up the body. It entwined itself about her chest and she finally saw its head.

The snake gazed towards the east several times, as much as to say to her that one must look to the east for God's guidance. For some strange reason, this snake also brought with it a feeling for love, goodness and peace.

The snake gradually withdrew, sliding down the left side of the bed toward the east and vanished.[3] The reason for this first vision, as it is understood by Jeane Dixon herself, is to prepare her for the ones which will follow.[4]

The second vision which constitutes a part of this visionary mosaic occurred six years later, on a rainy, dreary weekday morning in the year 1958. At the time of this vision, Jeane Dixon was standing in St. Matthew's Cathedral in front of the statue of the Virgin Mary for a time of meditation and prayers.

She was just preparing to light the candles for intentions, when she put her hands down in her purse for coins. Her hands became entangled in a large group of purple and gold balls. Suddenly the balls began to float upward, and finally merged into a large purple disc which had a gold edge. It encompassed the breast and head of the statue of the Virgin Mary, and her face came alive.

Then a bright light shone throughout St. Matthew's Cathedral. The Cathedral appeared to be filled with every kind of people and religion imaginable. Kings and queens, as well as the lowest of peasants, were present. Every nationality and creed could be found somewhere in the large crowd. Everyone was bathed in this same bright light which filled the Cathedral, and peace came over everyone present.[5]

Jeane Dixon's interpretation of this vision is the prediction that the Roman Catholic Church would soon bring all the religions and nationalities of the world together in a council at Rome. This she believes was fulfilled in the Ecumenical Council of Vatican II, summoned by the late Pope John XXIII.⁶ This was to be the first step for Jeane Dixon in her understanding of the relationship of this visionary mosaic to the future of the religion of the world.

The third of the four visions which comprise the mosaic took place later that year, once again in St. Matthew's Cathedral. This time Jeane Dixon was kneeling in prayer and holding her crystal ball. From the dome of the cathedral, a glorious bright light shone. There in the light stood the Virgin Mary, draped in purplish blue.

To her right and slightly above her was a cloud-like formation, in which Jeane Dixon was able to read the word "Fatima." There she saw the empty throne of the Pope; on one side was a Pope with his face bleeding, and there were many hands reaching out for the throne.

The interpretation of this according to Jeane Dixon is the prediction that in this century a Pope will suffer bodily harm. The insignia of the Pope will change; the power will no longer reside in the person of the Pope, even though the power will still be there.⁷

The final prophecy in Jeane Dixon's visionary mosaic is considered by her to be the most significant as well as the most soul-stirring vision of her life. It took place on February 5, 1962, shortly before the rising of the sun.

She was prepared for this most significant vision in the three days preceding February 5, 1962. On the first of these three days, Jeane Dixon was meditating in her room. Suddenly she was aware that the five lights in the crystal chandelier were dimming, and the lights finally went out. But there was, in the center of each of the lights, a strange brilliantly glowing round ball. Frightened by this event, she ran to Mr. Dixon's bedroom. He assumed that a fuse had blown, until he came to her room and now saw all the lights brightly burning.

Once again on the following evening, while Jeane Dixon was meditating, this strange phenomenon occurred. This time Jeane Dixon stared at the tiny glowing balls. She heard a small crackling noise, and the bulbs began to glow again, until normal lighting was restored.

Then again on the third night, this same phenomenon occurred.[8]

The following morning, February 5, 1962, Jeane Dixon was gazing out her bedroom window toward the east. Stepping out of the bright rays of the sun, she saw Queen Nefertiti and a Pharaoh. In the arm of the Queen was a baby, clothed in ragged, soiled garments.

To one side of the Queen, Jeane Dixon could catch a glimpse of a pyramid. The Pharaoh and the Queen came towards her and thrust the baby forward, which indicated that it was being offered by them to the whole world. From this baby, then, came forth bright rays of light. Because of the light, Jeane Dixon couldn't notice the Pharaoh in the background, but saw the Queen departing. The Queen then paused for a drink of water and was knifed in the back.

When Jeane finally shifted her attention back to the baby, he had already attained manhood. A small cross materialized above his head and grew larger. People from all religions, races and color came to worship him. They were all one.

The room became dark, and the vision vanished.

Jeane Dixon looked at her clock and noted the time at 7:17 a.m. (EST).[9]

The interpretation of this fourth vision of our mosaic, according to Jeane Dixon, is that on February 5, 1962, somewhere in the Middle East, at about 7 a.m. (EST) a child was born, who would unite all mankind into one new Christianity by the end of this century.

He is to be a descendant of Queen Nefertiti and her husband, the Pharaoh. He is also to be the answer to the problems of this world and its prayers. His force will be first realized in the early 1980's. He will solve the problem of war and restore peace to this world. In 1999, all people will understand the complete fulfillment of this great prophetic vision.[10]

Thus we have seen the substance of each of the visionary portions of this great prophetic mosaic, as well as the interpretation and understanding of it according to Jeane Dixon herself.

The first vision was to prepare her for the following three visions. The second vision was claimed to have been fulfilled in the Ecumenical Council of Vatican II. The third vision is futuristic, in that a Pope will suffer bodily harm, and that the insignia and power of the Pope will change. The fourth vision speaks of one who is already on the world scene, who will grow up to be our future world leader.

In her vision of this future world leader, Jeane Dixon saw Queen Nefertiti and her husband, the Pharaoh, bring a child forth to present to the world as an offering.

Nefertiti was the Queen of Egypt during the Eighteenth Dynasty. She was married to Pharaoh Amenhotep IV, often known in Egyptian history as the great "Heretic King." He was a great religious reformer, attempting to replace the old traditional form of Egyptian religion with a form of Sun worship; seeking to establish the cult of Aton. For that reason he changed his name to Ikhnaton (literally "He in whom Aton is satisfied"). He built a new capital in the desert called Tell-el-Amarna, which became a rival to the old capital at Thebes. His new religion collapsed in civil wars and died with the King. He is probably best remembered for the phrase "The solar disc is satisfied." One must note here that in the vision of Jeane Dixon, Queen Nefertiti and the Pharaoh returned back to them.

The Pharaoh who followed Ikhnaton was Tutankhaton (literally "image of Amon"), who was the son-in-law of Ikhnaton and Nefertiti. They had seven daughters, but no sons. Tutankhaton married Ikhnaton's third daughter and was probably about twelve years of age when he ascended the throne as Pharaoh. He was really a helpless puppet in the hands of the priests who were striving hard to exterminate his father-in-law's memory, and restore to Egypt the true religion which was worshipped in the past. Tutankhaton did restore the old religion and returned the political capital back to Thebes. He also changed his name to Tutankhamon (literally "image of Amon"), reverting back to the traditional religion of worshipping Amon.

An examination of the mummy found in his burial place shows that he was about eighteen years old at his death. Thus he probably reigned for about six years. One should note here in connection with Tutankhamon, that he was only the son-in-law of Queen Nefertiti and Pharaoh Ikhnaton. They had only daughters, and no sons. Therefore in the vision given to Jeane Dixon, the male

child presented does not bear a historical significance, but must have some other significance of
which we have no information, apart from what the
vision reveals.

But this future world leader of whom it is revealed in the vision would solve our problem of war
and bring peace, would be the answer to all the
prayers of a troubled world, and who will bring all
mankind in one all-embracing faith of a new Christianity, bears the resemblance of the one who is
spoken of in the Bible as being opposed to God, to
His kingdom, and His work. He is more commonly
known in Christianity as the Antichrist. He is not
on God's side as we are led to believe by Jeane
Dixon's vision, but he is opposed to God.

At the end of this present age, the Bible declares
that this man, in whom the embodiment of evil re-
sides, will appear on the world scene. Often in the
Bible he is known by other titles, such as "the little horn" in Daniel 7, the "King of the North" in
Daniel 11, the "Lawless One" and the "Man of
Sin" in II Thessalonians 2, and the "Beast" in Revelation 13.

The Antichrist is one in whom the world will follow and worship in one all-embracing faith. In this
regard he is likened to the future world leader in
Jeane Dixon's vision. He becomes the supreme religious object of the organized world and rules politi-
cally over the entire human race. Under his sup-
pressive rule, there will be no war, only peace for
all those who will worship him. "Through his poli-
cy he shall cause craft to prosper in his hand; and
he shall magnify himself in his heart, and by peace
shall he destroy many."[1] There will be a kingdom
of peace on this earth through the Antichrist, without God. He will enforce his persuasion of power

upon them by the exclusion from all commercial rights for those who do not accept the mark of the Beast signifying allegiance and worship to him.[12]

The Antichrist, being the religious object of worship, will also confirm a covenant with the Jews for seven years. Their religious worship will be restored, including the sacrificial system. After three and one-half years, he will cause the sacrifice to cease.[13]

He is not only involved with the Jews, but with every nation in the world. "Power was given him over all kindreds, and tongues, and nations. And all that dwell upon the earth shall worship him."[14] Now here is the great Ecumenical Christianity as revealed to Jeane Dixon in her vision. But note the religiosity of the persons who worship the Antichrist, the ones who are supposed to comprise this great "New Christianity." They are those "whose names are not written in the book of life of the Lamb slain from the foundation of the world."[15] This Ecumenical religion spoken of in the Bible is one that is in opposition to God and His Work. This certainly is not Christianity.

The Antichrist also has a false prophet working miracles for him in his presence, causing many people to believe in and worship Antichrist.[16] He will do great and wonderful miracles,[17] and will deceive many people by them.[18]

The Antichrist will be sitting in the Temple in Jerusalem, exalting himself to the position of Deity.[19] This one will the Lord Jesus Christ slay with the breath of His mouth at His Appearing.[20]

In conclusion, the world leader of the future as envisioned by Jeane Dixon, bears a great resemblance to the Antichrist, the future world leader who will oppose God.

In A *Gift of Prophecy*, Jeane Dixon clearly believes that this future world leader would be one "who will walk among the people to spread the wisdom of the Almighty Power."[21] He is portrayed as one who will represent God here on earth. In fact, Jeane Dixon becomes so involved in her vision that "she seemed to be in the very midst of the action, joining in the adoring worship" of this future world leader.

However, in her latest book, *My Life And Prophecies*, her prophecy of this future world leader has changed. Now she claims "he will form a new 'Christianity,' based on *his 'almighty power.'* "[23] Previously he would "spread the wisdom of *the Almighty Power*."[24]

Until September, 1969, she predicted this future world leader would represent God. Now she claims: "There is no doubt in my mind that the 'child' is the actual person of the Antichrist, the one who will deceive the world in Satan's name."[25]

NOTES

[1] Montgomery, Ruth, *A Gift of Prophecy,* New York: Bantam Books: 1966, page 181
[2] *Ibid.,* page 173
[3] *Ibid.,* pages 173-4
[4] *Ibid.,* page 175
[5] *Ibid.*
[6] *Ibid.,* page 176
[7] *Ibid.,* page 177
[8] *Ibid.,* page 179
[9] *Ibid.,* pages 180-1
[10] *Ibid.,* page 181
[11] Daniel 8:25
[12] Revelation 13:7, 11-18; 17:12-13
[13] Daniel 9:27

14 Revelation 13:17-18
15 Revelation 13:18
16 Revelation 13:12
17 Revelation 13:13
18 II Thessalonians 2:9-12
19 Daniel 11:36-39; II Thessalonians 2:3-4
20 II Thessalonians 2:8
21 Montgomery, Ruth, *Op. Cit.*, page 181
22 *Ibid.*, pages 180-181
23 Dixon, Jeane, and Noorbergen, Rene, *My Life And Prophecies,* page 180
24 Montgomery, Ruth, *Op. Cit.*, page 181
25 Dixon, Jeane, and Noorbergen, Rene, *Op. Cit.*, page 187

6. PROPHETESS OF GOD?

WE HAVE now arrived at the heart of the matter regarding Jeane Dixon and Biblical prophecy: Is she or is she not a prophetess of God in the true Biblical sense. This is an involved and complex subject containing multifarious elements.

According to the Bible, a prophet is an inspired person (II Peter 2:21), a spokesman for God (Exodus 4:10-16). That which they speak is prophecy, and prophecy can be defined in a twofold manner.

Prophecy can simply mean the foretelling of a given event of which knowledge has been imparted from God. An example of this would be the Old Testament prophecies of the birth, death and resurrection of Jesus Christ, as foretold by the Old Testament prophets.

Prophecy can also mean forthtelling the will of God in a specified discernable context as the Holy Spirit would reveal. In the New Testament, the prophet Agabus clearly portrays both roles. In Acts 11:28 he clearly foretells of a great famine "by the spirit," and in Acts 21:10-14 he forthtells the "will of the Lord" (v.14) in accord with "thus saith the Holy Ghost" (v.11).

Perhaps the first question one must face in this section is whether or not the gift of prophecy is available today for the Church. If the gift is not available today, then our answer regarding Jeane Dixon's prophetic abilities is relatively simple: she cannot be a prophetess of God. If the gift of prophecy is present today, then we must analyze it to see if she has the gift of prophecy as bestowed by the Holy Spirit (I Corinthians 12:7-10).

For some Christians, this question is easily answered because they do not believe the gift of prophecy is for the Church today. The basis for this view is generally found in I Corinthians 13:8-9, "Love never faileth: but whether there be prophecies, they shall fail; whether there be tongues, they shall cease; whether there be knowledge, it shall vanish away." While these verses are clearly stating that at some point in history the gift of prophecy will terminate, one must refer to the context to find out exactly when this will occur.

In the next verse Paul states, "But when that which is perfect is come, then that which is in part shall be done away." This verse is interpreted by them to mean the consummation of all spiritual gifts at either the completion of the New Testament Canon, or the end of the Apostolic era. Thus the gifts of the Spirit, including the gift of prophecy, ended in the early Church. This is the position which was popularized and virtually canonized by the late Benjamin B. Warfield, a great Christian scholar.

The classical interpretation of Historic Christianity has been the termination of the gifts of the Holy Spirit at the Second Coming of our Lord Jesus Christ. One can find a great deal of information on this in most scholarly and exegetical commentaries, which would support this position. Also, in most of the Bibles containing marginal notes, one can find references to other passages concerning the Second Coming, connected to I Corinthians 13:10.

This certainly is the contextual import as one proceeds to verse 12. "For now we see through a glass darkly; but then face to face: now I know in part, but then shall I know even as also I am known." This verse clarifies the interpretation of verse 10 as to when the gifts of the Spirit will cease. It is when we see "face to face" and when "we know even also as we are known." This cannot be separated from the concept of the Second Coming of Jesus Christ, at which time the gifts of the Spirit will no longer be necessary.

Since the gift of prophecy is available today, we must examine the evidence regarding it very carefully. This task would be simplified if we knew that all prophesying is of God, for then there would be no reason to question any prophet or prophetess. However, the facts in Scripture plainly state that not all spirits are of God. (I John 4:1-3) "Beloved, believe not every spirit, but try the spirits whether they are of God: because many false prophets are gone out into the world."

The Scriptures also reveal that these false prophets can predict the future to some extent, and even prophesy in the name of the Lord Jesus Christ. Jesus said, "Many will say to me in that day, Lord, Lord, have we not prophesied in thy name? and in thy name cast out devils? and in they name done wonderful works? And then will I profess unto them, I never knew you: depart from me, ye that work iniquity." (Matthew 7:22-23)

Jesus also spoke eschatologically of the false prophets in the last days, saying "false Christs and false prophets shall rise, and shall shew signs and wonders, to seduce, if it were possible, even the elect. But take ye heed: behold, I have foretold you all things" (Mark 14:22-23, cf Matthew 24:24).

The nature of the gift of prophecy is such that

there is an ever-present danger of false prophets. But one must also note that in I Corinthians 12 where the gift of prophecy is mentioned as bestowed upon by the Holy Spirit, the same is true of the gift of the "discerning of spirits" (I Corinthians 12:10). This gift is given to some by the Holy Spirit to enable them to recognize the truth or falsity of prophetic utterances. This gift is still bestowed by the Holy Spirit today, allowing some this gift to discern between truth and error.

Throughout the New Testament, the danger of impersonation even in the prophets is clearly taught and recognized, and in I John 4:2-3, a test prescribed to distinguish error from truth. The test is doctrinal in nature, dealing with the confession of the Person of our Lord Jesus Christ. Certainly the purpose of Biblical prophecy was to manifest God's power in glorifying His Person, in exalting His redemptive work in Jesus Christ, and setting forth the divine character of His Revealed Word.

Apart from divine revelation, man does not know what a day will bring forth. Only God knows the future as well as the past. "Known unto God are all the works from the beginning of the world" (Acts 15:18). Therefore it is the active supernatural power of God which reveals to the prophets the content of their discourses. The words they speak are not their own, but the message that God would have them proclaim.

It is quite clear in the Scriptures that the prophets or prophetesses of God are not free to follow their own inclinations. They are, instead, led by the hand of God (II Kings 3:15; Isaiah 8:11; Jeremiah 15:17; and Ezekiel 1:3). This is clearly the position of the New Testament also, as Peter states "prophecy came not in old time by the will of man, but holy men of God spake as they were moved by the Holy Ghost" (II Peter 1:21).

Jeane Dixon sincerely believes that "it is only God's spirit, working through her, that is responsible for her visions and prophecies."[1]

When a prophet or prophetess is moved by the Holy Spirit to speak, that prophecy must come to pass, for God cannot lie. His leading hand is there to protect His message. This is continually pointed out in the New Testament that events transpired "that it might be fulfilled which was spoken of the Lord by the prophet," and every such reference serves to emphasize the trustworthiness of the words of a true prophet.

This is not the case with Jeane Dixon, because she does not prophesy or predict in the name of the Lord, but merely attributes her abilities to God. Her record for prophetic accuracies is scarred with numerous inaccuracies, thereby negating the trustworthiness of her prophetic words as well as the claimed revelation from God.

Furthermore, the commission of the Old Testament prophets was to show the people their transgressions and sins. (Isaiah 58:1; Ezekiel 22:2; 43:10; and Micah 3:8). But in the prognostications of Jeane Dixon, whether foretelling or forthtelling, one finds almost nothing regarding the sins and transgressions of the people against God.

This is also revealed in the fact that the basic morality of the people was a great concern of the Old Testament prophets. They were preachers of the Law, ethics and morality. The Ten Commandments became their basis for morality revealing the Holiness of God and showing man his sinfulness before God. Instances of this occurred in the Old Testament times with Nathan confronting

King David regarding Bathsheba, and also in the prophet Elijah, opposing Ahab and Jezebel. Yet in the prophetic elements of Jeane Dixon's prophecies, one finds again almost nothing regarding this element.

The prophets of old continually warned the nation of Israel of God's coming judgment. This element of prophecy is seldom found in any of Jeane Dixon's prophecies. It is the clear teaching of Scripture that there is a coming judgment in which God will pour out His wrath on all who reject His Son and the sacrifice on the Cross of Calvary (Matthew 25:46; II Thessalonians 1:9; II Peter 2:9; and Revelation 20:11-15).

Another element of prophecy condemned in the Old Testament is the occultist's "bag of tricks," the various methods and channels used to obtain vibrations and prophetic information. Many of the channels used by Jeane Dixon are forbidden by Scripture.

Regarding the New Testament gift of prophecy, it is stated "he that prophesieth speaketh unto men to edification, and exhortation, and comfort . . . he that prophesieth edifieth the church" (I Corinthians 14:3-4). Prophets were a part of the church (Acts 13:1) and their task through the revelation of God was to build up the church, provide growth in Christian character, set forth ethical precepts and warnings, and encourage Christians through personal testimony and example. One does not find these elements in the prophetic utterances of Jeane Dixon.

Last, but not least, is the subject of the doctrine of God as understood by Jeane Dixon. Of this there is very little information available, apart from the known facts that she is a devout Roman

Catholic, that she reads the Twenty-Third Psalm every morning, and that she has attended Mass every morning of her life. Perhaps the only insight into this subject is to be found in a magazine interview with Jeane Dixon by Jerome Ellison. He wrote an article regarding this interview in *The Christian Herald*, March 1966, entitled "Jeane Dixon talks about God." Yet from this article, it is quite clear that her concept of God is not the same as the concept of God revealed in the Scriptures.

Jeane Dixon stated that "There is only one God and only one faith, but there are innumerable channels, and each must find the right one for him.'" What she is really saying here is that there is one "God," but many ways in which one can find God and have a relationship with Him.

She gives us an example of this by saying, "A Buddhist is going to recognize that One Power. So let us forget about such terms as 'interfaith'. Let everybody seek his own faith at the one Central Source.'" Buddhism provides an excellent example in illustrating Jeane Dixon's concept of God, because it is a religion in general which tends toward atheism, although some Buddhists do hold their leader Buddha to be god. Certainly this concept of God or lack of god is foreign to the Scriptures.

In her latest book, *My Life And Prophecies*, Jeane Dixon makes several references to Jesus Christ, His Incarnation and His Second Coming; the Trinity, the Holy Spirit, etc. Yet her understanding of Christianity remains clearly syncretistic. She still believes that all religions, Christian, Jew, Hindu, Buddhist are one under God. This will become evident in the future.' She also agrees with Thornton Wilder in his book *The Eighth Day*, when he stated "Religions are merely the garments of faith."[5]

Perhaps this syncretism can best be understood in the light of the following statement. "From the very moment we are conceived and receive life, we become a part of God."[6] If this is true, then we can see how she arrives at her belief that all religions are one.

The Scriptures declare that there is one God, and only one way in which mankind can have a personal relationship with Him. The apostle Paul writes, "For there is one God, and one mediator between God and men, the man Christ Jesus" (I Timothy 2:5). The apostle Peter confirms this by stating, "Neither is there salvation in any other: for there is none other name (Jesus Christ) under heaven given among men, whereby we must be saved" (Acts 4:12). This is verified by our Lord Jesus Christ Himself when He claimed to be "the way, the truth, and the life; no man comes to the father" except they come through Him.

The Scriptures contradict Jeane Dixon's concept of finding God through many different channels. There is only one way to have a personal relationship with God, and that is through His Son Jesus Christ.

In conclusion, when one examines the multifarious elements involved in Biblical prophecy, one finds Jeane Dixon coming short of the standard set by the Scriptures in the following elements of Biblical prophecy:

1) She has made numerous false predictions.

2) She does not prophesy in the name of the Lord.

3) She does not prophetically point out the sins and transgressions of the people against God.

4) She does not prophetically preach the Law, ethics and morality.

5) She does not prophetically declare and warn people of God's Coming Judgment upon those who reject Jesus Christ.

6) The Church is not edified, exhorted, and instructed by her gift of prophecy.

7) Many of the methods she uses to obtain vibrations and predictive information are forbidden in the Scriptures.

8) She does not proclaim Jesus Christ as the only way one can personally know God.

Is Jeane Dixon a prophetess of God? She certainly is not a prophetess by either the qualifications recorded in the Old Testament or the New Testament. Rather, it becomes apparent that she possesses extraordinary psychic powers which she certainly used for humanity.

Jeane Dixon herself answers the question in *A Gift of Prophecy*. It seems for many years Far Easterners have noted the marvelous lines in the hands of Jeane Dixon, and have proclaimed her to have great prophetic powers. But Jeane Dixon regards these proclamations as nonsense. She does not believe herself to be a prophetess.[7]

NOTES

[1] Dixon, Jeane, and Noorbergen, Rene, *My Life And Prophecies*, New York: Coward-McCann: 1969, page 13

[2] *Christian Herald*, March 1966, "Jeane Dixon Talks About God" by Jerome Ellison, page 42

[3] *Ibid.*, page 43

[4] Dixon, Jeane, and Noorbergen, Rene, *Op. Cit.*, page 52, cf page 55

[5] *Ibid.*, page 204
[6] *Ibid.*, page 193
[7] Montgomery, Ruth, *A Gift of Prophecy*, New York: Basic Books: 1966, page 57

Part II

INTRODUCTION

IN THIS age in which we live, there is great interest in the supernatural and the metaphysical; in that realm which exists above and beyond the realm of sense experience. Parapsychology, astrology, prophecy, Atlantis, and reincarnation are generating a great deal of excitement through various media.

One of the outstanding examples of the above is the great "sleeping prophet," the late Edgar Cayce (pronounced Kay-see), whose readings are becoming extremely popular today. His work is carried on by the Association for Research and Enlightenment of Virginia Beach, Virginia, as well as in numerous A.R.E. study groups throughout the United States.

Just a casual perusal of any bookstore or newsstand would reveal the numerous books available on Edgar Cayce. Such titles as *Edgar Cayce—The Sleeping Prophet*, *There Is a River*, *Venture Inward*, *Many Mansions*, *Edgar Cayce on Prophecy*, *Edgar Cayce on Atlantis*, and *Edgar Cayce on Reincarnation* point to the popularity of his readings and his message.

This book will seek to present and analyze the readings of Edgar Cayce and the teachings of the Association for Research and Enlightenment in the light of the Word of God, for they are indeed becoming a dangerous threat for the Church of Jesus Christ today.

The Christian must be on the alert in this age,

for there are those who use the vocabulary of Christianity and pretend to be her helpers, but yet insidiously infiltrate and seek to destroy the basic message of the Church; not by attack, but by reinterpretation and by infiltration of philosophy and mystery religions into the essential elements of the Gospel message.

1. LIFE OF EDGAR CAYCE

EDGAR CAYCE was born on March 18, 1877, on a farm near Hopkinsville, Kentucky, in Christian County. He was born into an old conservative Kentucky family; his father, Leslie, being a Justice of the Peace.

Some people believe the psychic powers of this family were manifest before Edgar Cayce's day, in the person of his grandfather, a farmer who would use two forks of a witch-hazel tree to find water.

When Edgar was about seven or eight years old, he had a clairvoyant experience which eventually changed the entire future of his life. He was outdoors, in a secluded little nook, when "there was a humming sound, and a bright light filled the glade where he usually hid to read the wonderful stories. As he looked up, he saw a figure in white, bright as the noonday light, and heard a voice: 'Your prayers have been heard. What would you ask of me, that I may give it to you?' 'Just that I may be helpful to others,' he replied, 'especially to children who are ill, and that I may love my fellow man.'"¹ This was the beginning of the visions of Edgar Cayce, and his ministry to help mankind.

Yet, in his youth, Edgar questioned his many dreams and visions. Once, when Dwight L. Moody, the great Evangelist, came to his area, Edgar met with him and discussed these experiences. Through this conversation, Edgar began to place more trust in such occurrences. As he grew up, people began to respect him and trust him because of his amazing psychic capacities, and he developed his "God-given" psychic abilities.

One day, Edgar suffered from a severe headache and wandered about the streets in an unconscious state. When he was found by a friend and brought home, he regained consciousness, but lost his voice. For twelve months he could hardly speak above a whisper. Edgar tells us what happened: "Among those who treated me was a hypnotist—not a physician, not a highly educated man—just a plain business man who was interested in the phenomenon of hypnotism. While under this influence, it was said, I was able to speak, yet when brought from under it, I could not. Successive attempts to hypnotize me seemed to 'get on my nerves.' I was unable to sleep, so this was discontinued for the time. As the experiments were witnessed by many, I received a good deal of newspaper publicity. A noted physician of New York visited me. Hypnotism was tried again, but this time, with no results. Then I told him of my experiences as a child, and that I felt sure that I could make myself unconscious for I felt within me the same condition taking place when being hypnotized as I felt when putting myself to sleep. He suggested that this was why the hypnotist was unable to give me post-suggestion, but if I would put myself in the unconscious condition and someone talk to me, I would be able to tell them the trouble and how to get rid of it. Can you imagine what that meant to my mind? When I think this over now I wonder why I haven't been called more names than I have.

"My parents, having little faith in hypnotism, were afraid to try this physician's suggestion. After several months I was unable to even whisper and many declared I had galloping consumption. I pled with my mother and father to at least let the man who had first hypnotized me try the experiment the specialist had suggested. They finally agreed. So on a Sunday afternoon, March 31, 1901, this man came to our home. No one was present except my mother, father, and this gentleman. I lay on the couch and gave the first of what is now called a 'reading.' In a few minutes I lost consciousness. They told me I said (after this man's suggestion that I would see myself):

" 'Yes, we can see the body. In the normal physical state this body is unable to speak, due to a partial paralysis of the inferior muscles condition producing a physical effect. This may be removed by increasing the circulation to the affected parts by suggestion while in this unconscious condition.'

"I am told that in five to ten minutes I said, 'It is all right.' Then the man told me to wake up at a given time. When I was conscious again I knew that I could speak. That was my first reading.'"

Since that first reading, some 30,000 readings have followed, in which he correctly predicted the sex of unborn infants; diagnosed and prescribed successful cures for epilepsy, diabetes, cancer, nervous disorders, pyorrhea, tuberculosis, hemorrhoids, appendicitis, hernias, hay fever, arthritis, common colds, etc.; he predicted in April of 1929 the stock market crash of that year, the ending of the Depression in 1933, and the future value of land at Cape Henry and Norfolk (which many people bought on Cayce's advice).

A photographer by trade, with only a grammar school education, his medical vocabulary (while under a self-induced trance) perplexed some Bostonian medical authorities. Cayce could also speak numerous foreign languages fluently while in his trance, a feat he was unable to accomplish in everyday life.

Edgar was always fully aware of his academic limitations. Once, at the Cayce Hospital, Edgar began a lecture on the Relativity of Force by stating: "Many times in a tobacco field I have seen a little worm making a tiny hole in a leaf. From his viewpoint he was doing the very best he could, but he was making an awful mess of the tobacco. I remind myself very much of that worm when I tackle a subject like this.'"

Edgar was purported to be a devout Protestant, one who prayed regularly to God, and had read the Bible through once every year for forty-six years. He was a Sunday school teacher as well as an active church member.

In 1922, the Cayce family moved to Virginia Beach, "a place designated in the psychic information many years before as the best location for the hospital.'" But Cayce's numerology also pointed to Virginia Beach as the best location, thereby providing a double proof.

EDGAR CAYCE of VIRGINIA BEACH
54719 31735 49979591 25138

26   19   53   19
8 & 10 — (9)   8 & 10 — (9)

This became the impetus for the founding of the Cayce Hospital. In May, 1927, this hospital was first incorporated as the Association of National Investigators and eventually became the Cayce Hospital for Research and Enlightenment. Today, it is known as the Association for Research and Enlightenment, a non-profit organization chartered in Virginia, which carries on the psychic research begun by Edgar Cayce.

Until the year 1923, Edgar had only given physical or health readings. Then he met Arthur Lammers, a printer from Dayton, Ohio, and began to trace the man's experience in his past lives through his readings. This was Cayce's introduction to what later became the center of his religious philosophy, as well as that of the Association for Research and Enlightenment: REINCARNATION and KARMA. Edgar had difficulty at first in accepting this but soon assimilated it as "Truth."

Tired and worn out, Edgar Cayce gave his last reading September 11, 1944—for himself. The readings had continually warned him not to "read" more than twice a day, or he would disintegrate. But with the problems of the world, a war in which his own two sons, Hugh Lynn and Edgar Evans, were fighting, requests for readings coming at the rate of fifteen hundred a day—with all this the humanitarian Edgar Cayce did seven or eight daily readings. At age 67, he had completely burned himself out for the cause of humanitarianism.

Edgar Cayce's reputation has survived him, and a small but rapidly growing cult has formed around his teachings. Many people are studying his readings (filled with medical, psychological, religious and metaphysical information) at the Association for Research and Enlightenment at Virginia Beach, Virginia, as well as at many A.R.E. centers throughout the United States. These readings are claimed to be "a body of ideas which in his lifetime changed people's lives and is now being progressively proved as potent to do the same today."[5]
Thus, Edgar Cayce, though dead, lives on in his readings.

NOTES

[1] Stearn, Jess, *Edgar Cayce—The Sleeping Prophet,* pp. 26-27
[2] Cayce, Edgar, *What I Believe*, pp. 7-8
[3] *Ibid.*, p. 2
[4] Cayce, Hugh Lynn, *Venture Inward,* p. 29
[5] *The Edgar Cayce Legacy,* p. 5

2. THE READINGS OF EDGAR CAYCE

ACCORDING TO the A.R.E., "Reading is a term used to describe the clairvoyant discourses which Edgar Cayce gave while in a self-induced hypnotic sleep-state."[1]

In the files at the A.R.E., there are volumes of readings for people to study. The readings are indexed and cross-referenced according to major subject headings in their card-catalogue. There are about 8,976 Physical Readings dealing with the realm of health and medicine; 2,500 Life Readings (all about the past lives of people); 799 Business Readings; 667 Readings concerning the interpretation of dreams; 401 Readings dealing with the mental and spiritual realm; 24 Readings concerned with marriage and the home; and 879 miscellaneous Readings.

Edgar Cayce gave his first Reading concerning his loss of voice control. He diagnosed the problem and prescribed a cure for it. The cure worked. He developed a set procedure in giving his readings: "The first step in giving a reading is this: I loosen my clothes—my shoelaces, my necktie, my shirt-cuffs, and my belt—in order to have a perfect free-flowing circulation.

"Then I lie down on the couch in my office. If the reading is to be a physical one, I lie with my head to the south and my feet to the north. If it is to be a life reading, it is just the opposite: my feet are to the south, my head to the north. The reason for this difference is 'polarization,' as the readings themselves call it. I do not know. Once lying comfortable, I put both hands up to my forehead, on the spot where observers have told me that the third eye is located, and pray.

"Interestingly enough, I have unconsciously and instinctively, from the beginning, adopted the practices used by initiates in meditation. This instinctive putting of my hands to the point midway between my two eyes on my forehead is a case of what I mean.

"Then I wait for a few minutes, until I receive what might be called the 'go signal'—a flash of brilliant white light, sometimes tending towards the golden in color. This light is to me the sign that I have made contact. When I do not see it, I know I cannot give the reading. After seeing the light I move my two hands down to the solar plexus, and—they tell me—my breathing now becomes very deep and rhythmic, from the diaphragm. This goes on for several minutes. When my eyes begin to flutter closed (up till now they have been open, but glazed) the conductor knows I am ready to receive the suggestion, which he proceeds to give me, slowly and distinctly. If it is a physical reading, for example, the name of the individual to receive the reading is given to me, together with the address where he will be located during that period of time. There is a pause—sometimes so long a pause (they tell me) that it seems I haven't heard the directions, so they give them to me again—after which I repeat the name and address very slowly, until the body is located, and a description of its condition is begun.

"This, then, is how I give a reading. I am entirely unconscious throughout the whole procedure. When I wake up I feel as if I had slept a little bit

too long. And frequently I feel slightly hungry—
just hungry enough for a cracker and a glass of
milk, perhaps."[2]

While Edgar Cayce was in his self-induced
trance, giving a reading, someone asked him the
question "Who is giving this discourse?" He answered, "Are ye curious? Are ye serious? Look
within self."[3]

But this is a good question. One can clearly note
that when Edgar Cayce speaks in his trance, he
speaks in the first person "we," which suggests demonology as a possible source for the readings.

The readings were given in the presence of several people, one of whom was his secretary and ste-
nographer, Gladys Davis (now Mrs. Gladys Davis
Turner). The readings generally began with a discourse on a given subject, allowing time for questions and answers after the discourse. Gladys
Davis would transcribe what was said during the
readings, and these records are preserved in the
files of the A.R.E.

The readings are to be used today to help mankind. Cayce said they were "a body of ideas which
in his lifetime changed people's lives and is now
being progressively proved as potent to do the
same today."[4] For example, the A.R.E. circulates
the famous "Black Book" which contains many
home remedies for whatever ails you from baldness
to stuttering, collected and indexed from the actual
readings given by Cayce to be applied to our lives.

Much is said regarding the extensive usage of
Biblical terminology in the readings, a factor not
inharmonious with Cayce's yearly reading the
Bible through for forty-six years. One can also notice many similarities between Plato's *Atlantis* and
the material on the lost continent of Atlantis in the

readings of Edgar Cayce. The concept of the records of past experiences of the soul being written on the subconscious of the individual is very similar to Carl Gustav Jung's concept of the collective unconscious. His concept of reincarnation and Karma is nothing new in the realm of religion and philosophy.

While the material at the A.R.E. presents Edgar Cayce as fantastically accurate, almost to the point of infallibility in his medical diagnosis and treatments, prophecies and predictions, etc.—one must bear in mind an important fact: these records are preserved by his followers, who would naturally extol his accuracies.

It is claimed that Edgar Cayce wrongly diagnosed the symptoms of Dr. J. B. Rhine's three-year-old daughter. The followers of Edgar Cayce reply that this occurred in several instances because people did not always follow exactly the recommendations given in his readings.

Despite the defense by the A.R.E. and the followers of Edgar Cayce, it was Edgar Cayce himself who wrote: "Is the information through these readings a cure-all? No. For, some years ago, my mother, the most wonderful mother a man ever had, passed on. During the last few hours of her illness, she called me to her bed. I will always remember her words: "Son, your mother is going now. You have kept her alive for years through your work. Now she must go, but you must so live your own life that you may bring to others that comfort, that ease, which has so often come to your mother through those readings in which God speaks to those who will listen.' " The Readings were not a cure-all, not even to the great "medical genius."

NOTES

1. *Astrology and the Edgar Cayce Readings,* p. 1
2. *What I Believe,* pp. 21-22
3. Reading 5749-10
4. *The Edgar Cayce Legacy,* p. 5
5. *What I Believe,* p. 12

3. THE MEDICAL GENIUS OF EDGAR CAYCE

EPILEPSY, ULCERS, diabetes, gall bladder condition, cancer, nervous disorder, pyorrhea, tuberculosis, hemorrhoids, appendicitis, hernias, hay fever, arthritis, common colds, etc.—these are only a few of the medical problems which confronted the "medical genius" of Edgar Cayce. He not only diagnosed such medical problems while in a self-induced trance, but also prescribed fantastic cures of the home-remedy type.

For instance, his prescription for the cure of epilepsy called for a mixture of peanut oil, rubbed on in a certain pattern as given in the readings. For diabetes, a massage utilizing peanut oil exclusively was prescribed.

The A.R.E. published *The Black Book*, containing many home remedies from the readings of Edgar Cayce, to be used as cures today.

The focal point of Cayce's medical genius is his prescribed cure for cancer. The readings on cancer have been well researched in the files of the A.R.E., and great interest has focussed on one of the methods of treatment he has set forth. In line with his home-remedy-type cures, Cayce prescribed the use of a serum made from the blood of a rabbit. This method of treatment was used in only five of the seventy-eight cases concerning cancer. It was prescribed for glandular cancer, cancer of the thyroid, and cancer of the breast.

According to Edgar Cayce, the anti-cancer serum is made by taking pus from the person to be cured, injecting this into the rabbit's shoulder. The infection caused by this will form the serum to be used. This information was from a reading given in 1926. In 1930, Edgar Cayce added cattle as a potential source for the anti-cancer serum.

It is claimed that in April, 1966, at the Wayne State University in Detroit, a team of researchers discovered a potential cure for cancer, using a serum formulated by the interaction of the patient's own cancer cell with the blood of a rabbit.

Of course, the questions so often asked remain to be answered: Where did Edgar Cayce get this medical information from? What is the source of this "medical genius"? Edgar Cayce said, "I am convinced from what the readings have repeated again and again that all healing comes from the divine within. Then what does the mind have to do with healing? It has to be awakened, either by something without or by something within, to that consciousness that the healing is from within, not from without."[1] It is from the divine within that the readings of Edgar Cayce come forth—from this his medical genius is developed, and from this the fascinating prophecies have their origin.

NOTES

[1] *What I Believe*, p. 26

4. THE PROPHECIES OF EDGAR CAYCE

WHEN IT comes to foretelling the future, there are very few who can approach the greatness of the "sleeping prophet." Jess Stearn (a one-time skeptic regarding Cayce and A.R.E.), now a convert, attributes a fantastic accuracy to the prophecies of Edgar Cayce.[1]

Edgar Cayce, conscious or unconscious, envisioned events which would take place as predicted. One day he received a vision while in his garden. Dropping his hoe, he ran inside and locked himself in his study. Several hours later he emerged from his study, and told of the vision he had had in which millions would die in the forthcoming World War II. This instance occurred shortly before the War began.

The A.R.E. together with the many followers of Edgar Cayce claim that he had correctly foreseen (through visions and readings) just about every major crisis in the world, from World War I through World War II.

Some of the prophecies of Edgar Cayce, being very vague and general, were interpreted in the light of the then current events. There were also numerous specific prophecies which came true during his lifetime and even afterward. And then there are those prophecies which are futuristic—which, according to Edgar Cayce, will come to pass.

In April of 1929, Edgar Cayce predicted the stock market crash of that year. He not only predicted the Great Depression, but also predicted the ending of the Depression in 1933. He predicted that the land in the area of Cape Henry and Norfolk would one day be valuable, because these towns would become leading seaports. There were several people who actually bought this land on the advice of Edgar Cayce and made money on it when the prophecy came true. "All I did was follow Cayce," one said.

Edgar Cayce's prophecies have great import for today. Beginning in January, 1934, the prophecies declared: During the period from 1958-98 there will be many earth-shaking events, due to a solar shift. The inner core of the earth has been in a turmoil since 1936, but the signs of this inner turmoil were not to be noticed until 1958. So from 1958-1998, we will see the results of the solar shift. There will be physical changes on several continents. The greater portion of the island of Honshu will sink into the sea. There will be tremendous upheavals in the regions of the Arctic and the Antarctic. There will be great volcanic eruptions in the Torrid Zone.

On the west coast of America, Los Angeles and San Francisco will be destroyed and will slide into the Pacific Ocean. On the east coast, New York will be destroyed and will slide into the Atlantic Ocean. The lost continent of Atlantis will rise from the ocean floor during this period (which will extend to the end of the century, when a millennium will be established).

Cayce in his readings connects the future of the earth (as it is now known) with the former continent of Atlantis. In one 1934 reading he designates the last four decades of the present century as being the period "when his light will again be seen in the clouds.'" The Biblical student will immediately tend to associate these words with passages dealing with the Second Coming of Christ.³ A careful study, however, will reveal striking differences as well as some similarities.

During these four Decades, there will be startling physical and climatic changes. Sometime this year or next,⁴ Poseidia (or some portion of this island, one of the islands which constituted Atlantis at the time of its final disaster) will be part of the first portions of Atlantis to rise again. Poseidia or at least this portion of it seems to be located in the area of the Bahamas, around Bimini. As part of the resurrection of Atlantis, there comes sweeping destruction to another land which will bear similarities to the first destruction of Atlantis.⁵ This will occur about 1976,⁶ with its initial stages beginning in 1968 or 1969. Proof (or evidence) for the discerning will be "the breaking up of some condition in the South Sea⁷ . . . and . . . the sinking or arising of that which is almost opposite to it, or in the Mediterranean, and the Aetna (Etna?) area."⁸ This will mark the commencement of the drastic climatic and physical changes which are to occur in the earth.

Many physical changes will happen; some will be major, others minor. The greatest changes will affect the North Atlantic Seaboard.⁹ Many portions of it will be disturbed. Portions of the east coast, of New York, perhaps New York City itself, will rather completely disappear. This will happen in another generation,¹⁰ and even earlier the southern portions of Carolina and Georgia will disappear.¹¹ Not only is the east coast affected, but the west coast and central portions of the United States will be disturbed and vast portions will cease to exist—at least in the form now known.

The Great Lakes will empty into the Gulf of Mexico instead of the Atlantic Ocean via the Saint Lawrence. Los Angeles and San Francisco will be under water before New York is affected. The safest portions of North America seem to be Virginia Beach, portions of Ohio, Indiana, and Illinois, and the Southern and Eastern part of Canada.[12] Land will appear off the east coast of America in the Atlantic and also in the Pacific Ocean.[13] The Arctic regions will also have upheavals and Greenland will become covered with the ocean. There will be volcanic eruptions in the torrid zones and South America will be shaken up in its entirety. There will be "in the Antarctic off Tierra Del Fueso, land, and a strait with rushing waters."[14]

In addition the American Continent, and the earth in other portions of the world will also be broken up. The greater part of Japan will sink into the ocean, and the upper part of Europe will change as in "the twinkling of an eye."[15] Current coast-lines will be the beds of oceans and many of the battlegrounds of 1941 will be "the seas, the bays, the land over which the new order will carry on their trade as one with another."[16] The poles of the earth will shift, and frigid and semi-tropical areas will become more tropical; the moss and the fern will grow.[17] Truly, if what Cayce predicts actually happens, there will be "new heavens and a new earth."

While the fulfilled prophecies of Edgar Cayce (as presented by the A.R.E.) appear to be virtually infallible, they do not claim infallibility for Edgar Cayce. Hugh Lynn Cayce, his son, tells us that ESP and psychic powers are by no means infallible.[18] Even Jess Stearn, in his book, *Edgar Cayce—The Sleeping Prophet*, is willing to concede that Edgar Cayce may have erred regarding the motivations of Adolf Hitler, whom he considered in the beginning to be essentially good.[19]

Back in 1943, Edgar Cayce did a reading for a publisher who was on his way to China. He predicted that within the next twenty-five years, China would definitely lean toward Christianity. 1968 is the test year for this prophecy, but in case it did not come to pass in 1968, the A.R.E. is prepared with several reasonable alternatives as to why it was apparently not fulfilled: One would be that the event took place, but that we will not see the fruits of it immediately. Another possibility would be that this event was prayed away without ever materializing. In other contexts, "praying away" was often mentioned by Cayce as effective.

No matter how hard some try to rationalize the apparent failure of any prophecy—whether they are right or not—the fact remains that Edgar Cayce was not considered as absolutely infallible by his followers. This is a most important point to remember concerning all his prophecies. While we know the Bible declares the test of true prophecy to be its fulfillment,[20] we likewise know that some of the prophecies of Edgar Cayce are therefore not "true" prophecies according to Biblical definition.

We know that God is absolutely infallible and thus cannot err;[21] that any true prophet of God, declaring the message of the Lord, cannot err.[22] Therefore, Edgar Cayce is not, by Biblical definition, a prophet of God; and his interpretation of Christian doctrine bears witness to this.

NOTES

[1] *Edgar Cayce—The Sleeping Prophet,* p. 81
[2] Reading 3976-15
[3] Matthew 24:30; Daniel 7:13; Revelation 1:17
[4] *Vid.* Reading 958-3
[5] Reading 3209-2
[6] Since a generation is approximately 33 years and since the reading was given in 1943, the time appears to be 1976
[7] i.e. The South Pacific
[8] Reading 311-8
[9] Note the words "Watch New York," reading 311-8
[10] Reading 1152-11, date 1941 plus 33 equals 1974
[11] Reading 1152-11
[12] *Ibid.*
[13] *Vid.* Readings 1152-11 and 3976-15
[14] Reading 3976-15
[15] *Ibid.,* cf I Corinthians 15:52
[16] Reading 1152-11
[17] *Vid.* Reading 3976-15
[18] *The Daily News,* Dec. 29, 1967, p. 6
[19] *Edgar Cayce—The Sleeping Prophet,* p. 81
[20] Deuteronomy 18:15
[21] Matthew 5:48
[22] II Peter 1:21

5. EDGAR CAYCE ON ATLANTIS

SINCE THE time Plato wrote his *Timaeus* and/or his *Critias*, men have dreamed of a lost island-continent, located in the Atlantic Ocean between Gibraltar and the American coast. According to Plato, an earlier Greek named Solon had talked with several Egyptian priests at Sais. They informed him that this large island had sunk overnight into the ocean some nine thousand years earlier or about 9600 B.C. Over the centuries, a large body of literature on this subject has developed, and recently great interest in the subject has arisen because certain scientists believe that they may have found Atlantis in a Mediterranean Island which sank into the sea c. 1400 B.C.[1]

According to Edgar Evans Cayce, the younger son of the famous "Sleeping Prophet," 664 of the 2500 life readings refer to Atlantean incarnations; moreover, "some refer to more than one relating to the same person, making a total of 700 Atlantean incarnations, approximately 30 percent of the total life readings given."[2] He indicates that he believes that further study will reveal the percentage to be fifty or more.[3] In about 68 percent of the Atlantean readings, the individual's name in his previous life in Atlantis is given.

The earliest life reading which contains a reference to Atlantis was given on November 20, 1923, and the last one (now known) on September 26, 1944—a period of about twenty-one years. The chief difficulty in interpreting these readings lies in the fact that so very few dates were given; around sixty percent either are dated or can be associated with one of the three destructions which Cayce states occurred in the Atlantean land(s). The remaining forty percent are not dated and cannot be easily associated with any particular time or period. Another related difficulty lies in the vast period of time covered (from c. 10,500,000 B.C. to 10,000 B.C.) and in the fact his Atlantean readings commence with that very vague and incompletely known period of the origins of mankind.

These Atlantean readings agree and disagree with the account by Plato. Examples of agreement are: Both described *Atlantis* at times as composed of islands and at other times as a single unit, and both associate the word, *Poseidon*, with Atlantis. Plato considers Poseidon to be a person, and Cayce used the root as the name of one of the Atlantean Islands, Poseidia. Perhaps the most striking disagreement refers to the disappearance of Atlantis. Plato states that Atlantis disappeared beneath the sea after a single day and night of rain; whereas the Cayce readings clearly indicate that Atlantis was destroyed by volcanic and earthquake-like types of activity in three distinct and widely separated events. Moreover, each of the destructions lasted over a period of months or even years, not days or a single day. The first of these periods of disaster seems to have happened about 50,700 B.C., the second, about 28,000 B.C., and the last around 10,000 B.C. The readings also indicate that warnings were given and that many inhabitants escaped prior to each disaster to Europe, Africa and the Americas.

*Atlantis From Around 10,000,000 B.C. to
Approximately 50,000 B.C.*

The life readings indicate in very vague and general terms the conditions of the surface and of the climate of the earth about ten and one half million years ago.[4] In one reading, Cayce states that in Europe and in Asia, only Norway, the Sahara, Tibet, Mongolia, and Caucasia had appeared as land masses; in South America, only southern Cordilleras and Peru; and in North America, Utah, Arizona, and Mexico.[5] In another reading, the land masses are enlarged to include Carpathia (the Garden of Eden),[6] Nevada, the Atlantic coastline of North America, the Andean or Pacific coast of South America, and the Urals.[7] In addition the continent-islands of Atlantis and Lemuria were in existence. Lemuria is usually located in the Pacific Ocean, opposite South America, yet he states that at this time it had for its western portion the Andean or Pacific coast of South America.[8] Perhaps this was after it had been partially destroyed?[9] Atlantis was situated in the area of the Atlantic Ocean between the Gulf of Mexico and the Mediterranean Sea;[10] it included the present Atlantic seaboard as its coastline and was about the size of Europe.[11] Other physical changes include the direction of the flow of the Nile; its direction was not to the North but toward the Atlantic Ocean into which it emptied. The waters of Tibet and Caucasia entered the North Sea; those from Mongolia flowed into the Pacific; and "those in the Plateau" entered the Northern Seas.[12] The present Mississippi Valley was then all ocean; in fact, the oceans were all turned about and bore different names.

Compared to the present, the climate also was

changed. The desert lands of the Sahara and of
Mongolia were fertile, and at least the former was
inhabited. The Urals and the northern portions of
the earth were tropical lands.

Unquestionably, one of the most startling statements concerns the origin of the human species.
Already, one hundred thirty-three million souls existed, and a half a million years later, one individual left, in the mounds and caves of northwestern
New Mexico, a permanent record—some draw-
ings.[13] From these statements, the conclusion that
man's origin was still earlier seems inescapable, but
it is precisely here where Cayce becomes vague and
obscure. Although the exact time and manner of
man's appearance is uncertain, some facts do
emerge. The earth was inhabited by animals before
it was by human beings (at least before they
dwelled on the earth in a physical form),[14] and
Adam was not the first human being.[15] In some
manner, there departed from the creative force(s)
or God, entities which were in some manner a part
of God and at the time distinct from God. He describes these early inhabitants of Atlantis as
"thought forces" and speaks of "thought bodies"
which gradually assumed form.[16] Elsewhere, he indicated that the Sons of God, in particular Amilius, an early Atlantean and a forerunner of Adam,
took an unspecified length of time to construct
their physical forms.[17] He classifies these early
people as Sons of God and/or of the Creative
Force, Sons of Belial, and daughters of men.[1]
Concerning the origins of mankind, he indicates
that both the "thought forces" or "bodies" and the
physical bodies of men had an evolutionary development.[19] Later, at an unspecified time, in five different places (Atlantis, Gobi, Africa, Carpathia,

and the Andes) a simultaneous projection[20] of the
thought forms into the developed physical ones.[21]
In this way, man arose as five different races[22] and
colors (red,[23] yellow, black, white, and brown, respectively[24]), not as an original pair. Each of the
races was associated, respectively with a different
"sense"; namely, touch, hearing, appetites, vision,
and smell.[25] The number five was selected because
it "represents man in his physical form and the attributes to which he may become conscious from
the elemental or spiritual to the physical consciousness."[26] Apparently, the "thought forces"
projected themselves at times into non-human
forms; moreover, the "human forms" were either
not fully developed or else they became defective.
In any case, their bodies gradually lost feathers
from their legs, hairs from their bodies, and tails
and/or other tuberances, claws and/or paws
were changed to hands and feet.[27] Although this
account of the origin of man bears some resemblance to the theory of evolution, it obviously differs radically from both the evolutionary and the
Biblical accounts.[28]

Were the one hundred thirty-three million souls
"thought forms" or had they already acquired
physical, human-type form? Were the inhabitants
of the earlier continents of Lemuria and of Da only
animals? Or were they human also? If so, were
these humans "thought forms" only or did they
also have physical forms? In the readings available
to this author, Cayce does not appear to have answered these questions unambiguously. This hazi-
ness and uncertainty extends to the events which
follow the appearance of man in Atlantis on down
to the first group of upheavals which terminated in
the first major destruction of the land masses of

Atlantis. These early Atlantean, pre-Adamic men, are described as being thought projections and also as having a physical being in which both sexes, male and female, were present in the same "body."[29] Already they had many of the characteristics which are associated with physical human bodies; e.g., one was a musician who played on pipe and/or reed instruments.[30] Corruption from the pure ways of God or the Creative Force(s) soon set in; many of the thought projections, after they had assumed matter or material form, began to engage in acts of self-indulgence.[31] These physically-encased, thought-projections gradually separated into two groups: those who followed the Law of One and the Sons of Belial.[32] The former had a standard which was the soul given by the Creator and were the offspring of the pure race or members of the original Sons of God who remained more or less pure. The Sons of Belial, however, rejected all standards except that of self, self-aggrandizement and self-indulgence, enjoyed all the pleasures of excesses, introduced the daughters of the children of the Law of One to these pleasures,[33] and diverted spiritual laws, constructive devices, and the like to material gain.[34] These two groups remind the Biblical student of the descendants of Seth and of Cain. Moreover, like the Biblical period before the Deluge, the Sons of the Creative Force looked upon the changed forms or the daughters of men with resulting corruption, pollution,[35] contempt, hatred, bloodshed, and lack of respect for others;[36] gigantic human forms existed;[37] and men lived for long periods of time, five hundred to a thousand years old. As time proceeded, very few of the original Sons of God remained true to their original ideals and purposes. The people became increasingly corrupt so that "every imagination of the thoughts of his heart was only evil continually" (Gen. 6:5) might truly be said of them.

Somewhere within this period of time, one of the Sons of God, Amilius, who had participated in the fashioning of his body, also participated in the separation of the sexes so that the offspring became male or female (not having both as they formerly did).[38] During the period in which the separation of the sexes had begun and the time in which the ten to twelve foot well-proportioned giants existed, Adam, the most ideal, appeared "as five in one—See?"[39] From what Cayce says, Adam appears to have been bisexual at the time.

The early Atlanteans lived in groups but not as households or families.[40] They had priests, royal persons,[41] laborers, producers, farmers, artisans,[42] time keepers,[43] and a most interesting and puzzling group which Cayce describes as "things" or "mere machines."[44] One of the divisions between the Sons of the Law of One and the Sons of Belial was over the treatment and use of these "things."

Gradually there arose in Atlantis a "kingdom" which surpassed all historic empires or civilizations, apparently including our own, in its scientific and economic achievements; it apparently lasted some two hundred thousand years.[45] They had aircraft,[46] balloon-type transportation,[47] submarines,[48] elevators,[49] and broadcasting systems similar to those of today.[50] The aircraft, and submarines were used for destructive purposes as well as beneficial ones. Other dual-purpose discoveries included a death-ray or supercosmic ray,[51] explosives (perhaps of the atomic variety),[52] radioactive forces and atomic energy.[53] According to the readings, today we are just rediscovering the power which they used for modes of travel and the natural forces they used in increasing their crops for individual consumption.[54] They also were better able to tap the energies of the sun for beneficial and destructive purposes.

As the Atlanteans were increasing in knowledge and in corruption, men began to give their rulers destructive forces. These destructive forces combined with the forces of nature precipitated the beginnings of the upheavals[55] which culminated in the first destruction of Atlantis.[56] At this time, volcanic eruptions occurred and the area of land which now lies below the Sargasso Sea disappeared.[57] As a result, the first exodus of people from Atlantis came about and the legends of the Garden of Eden arose.[58] This disaster seems to have taken place some seventy-five hundred years prior to the terminal phases of Atlantis' first disintegration.[59]

The only dated event which may be associated with the first Atlantean continental destruction was the summit meeting of the nations of the world held 50,722 B.C.[60] The occasion was the invasion of Atlantis by the giant members of the animal kingdom. The decisions of the nations and the results of their actions are not clear; they attempted to change the environment of the animals by the use of death rays or super-cosmic rays.[61] The Sons of Belial appear to have misused their knowledge in the attempts to destroy the invading animal life.[62] In spite of their efforts, the animals were destroyed by the activities of God, ice, and nature in the changing of the poles.[63] Whether this shift of the poles and whether this event is to be associated with the first of the changes in the land masses of Atlantis is not known; the emigrations to South and Central America, Egypt, Spain, and Portugal are the result of the warnings and the events which preceded this first destruction.[64]

Atlantis From Around 50,000 B.C. to About 20,000 B.C.

The effects and the extent of the first Atlantean Disaster was such that the continent was broken up into five islands.[65] On each occasion when Atlantis underwent disaster, its civilization was very advanced and scientific. Great progress had been made; it was a time of expansion, especially in the areas of the sciences, conveniences and transportation.[66] By the time of the second disintegration, the Atlanteans were able to travel in every element: air, water, and on land. Not only did they have aircraft, but they also had guided craft as well.[67] Communication was highly developed; they possessed varied means of carrying messages to other nations. Radio and television[68] appear to have become commonplace, being used for pleasure, communication, and for guiding (or assisting in the guidance) of the means of transportation. The Atlanteans enjoyed all our modern developments and even some which our current technologists have not rediscovered;[69] e.g., knowledge in the areas of mechanics, electricity, chemistry, photography, the overcoming of gravity, ability to read inscriptions through obstacles, such as walls, even at a distance, art and decorative work, atomic power plants, and x-rays.[70] Machines, lasers, and masers had been constructed and were used for many beneficial uses;[71] e.g., the rejuvenation of the human body. These expansions were not all in the material area, but also included the acquisition of "psychical" abilities. Cayce specifically mentions two of these: telepathy[72] and "astral" mobility.[73]

The social, economic, and religious organizations appear to be very similar to the conditions prior to the first disaster. The governmental structure was that of a kingdom; it had the usual hierarchy of governmental officials; e.g., ambassadors[74] and princes.[75] The people themselves had the occupations which would be anticipated; these included electrical engineers,[76] musicians,[77] navigators,[78] radio and television technicians, producers, and engineers,[79] psychology teachers,[80] and artists and artisans of all varieties.[81] They also possessed a priesthood[82] and the group which Cayce refers to as "things."[83] The people still possessed a variety of physical forms; i.e., they appear to have those who were bisexual, co-existing with those of the single sex variety.[84] Moreover, the people were separated into those who followed the Law of One and the Sons of Belial.[85]

As prior to the first disaster, the Atlanteans gradually became decadent,[86] disputes arose between the followers of the Law of One and the Sons of Belial,[87] and distinctions between the two groups became indistinct.[88] As earlier, one of the disputes was over the use of the group which Cayce terms, "things." Should they be used as beasts of burden, workers in clay, in mills? Some appear to have aided them in their evolutionary development;[89] others preferred to exploit them.[90] They became selfish,[91] interested in self-aggrandizement and self-indulgences, and applied the spiritual laws to material things.[92] Thus they utilized some of the constructive forces for destructive purposes.[93] Although the people appear to have had repeated and ample warnings of the impending disaster,[94] yet the majority seemed to have ignored them and continued to misuse their knowledge and power. Hence the disaster inevitably overtook them[95] because of failure to heed the warnings, because of the outbreak of rebellion[96] and because of the activities of the Sons of Belial.

The warnings and the destruction itself produced an exodus of people from Atlantis to various portions of the world, including the lands of Mayra (now called Nevada and Colorado) and Peru.[98] The upheavals and "volcanic-type" activity[99] resulted in the loss of some land masses and the separations of the continent into islands[100] and in climatic changes.[101] The date of this destruction is 28,000 B.C. or twenty-two thousand years before the Egyptian activity.[102]

Atlantis From 28,000 to About 10,000 B.C. The Time of the Final Disaster

After the second disturbance, the Atlanteans were forced to make many adjustments to the new conditions which they faced.[103] The scientific achievements were considerable, although they do not appear to be as advanced as in the earlier ages.[104] They still enjoyed many modern conveniences, used the forces of heat, power, and electricity,[105] and possessed the knowledge of gases, liquid air, and explosives.[106] They traveled extensively over the entire world[107] in airplanes, ships, and in land vehicles; they enjoyed a thriving world trade, especially with India, China, and Indo-China.[108] In the field of medicine, they made great discoveries[109] and constructed something resembling the modern hospital.[110] They were able to preserve physical life,[111] to regenerate the bodies of the "things"[112] and even to attempt to alter the future generations.[113] In the medical area they achieved such success that they were able to control people by means of electrical and mechanical devices.[114] Around this time they began to practice cremation.[115] In addition to the "hospitals," they also built recreation halls and schools, including ones to prepare teachers and ambassadors.[116]

The Atlanteans were classified and grouped according to their services;[117] they were employed in many diverse occupations, such as, engineers,[118] mathematicians,[119] chemists[120] and other scientists,[121] psychologists[122] and psychoanalysts, [123] vocational counsellors,[124] educators,[125] dam constructors,[126] stone cutters,[127] metal workers, workers in precious stones,[128] miners, trade merchants, artists and artisians,[129] dress designers,[130] agriculturists,[131] overseers and foremen,[132] historians,[133] musicians,[134] etc. Not only were material conditions very modern, but these mental and physical changes enabled men to live more productive lives and to be brought closer to the Creative Force(s) or God.[135] Even for the "things," this was a period of progress and of hope; the Atlanteans aided them in the elimination of the mental and physical hindrances to their development.[136]

The previous disasters had left Atlantis as a group of islands, the chief ones being called, Poseidia, Aryan, and Og,[137] and in a "perpetual" state of turmoil and rebellion.[138] The dissension between the Sons of the Law of One and the Sons of Belial[139] did not lessen; in other words, those who were of one faith contended with those who worshipped idols.[140] As time proceeded, the situation did not improve; at the time of the final destruction there was considerable internal corruption. The people could aptly be described as a "stiffnecked and adulterous people."[141] Eventually the Sons of Belial instigated the disaster by using destructive forces.[142] The destruction itself may have been rather sudden, but there were many warnings of the impending events.[143] Those who were wise heeded these warnings and emigrated to various places of the world:[144] Egypt,[145] the Spanish and Portuguese, Pyrenees,[146] the Mayan Yucatan,[147] Peru,[148] Central America,[149] Arizona, southern portions of California, southern New Mexico and Mexico.[150] Many of the readings give details concerning these migrations (not only these but also the earlier ones), mention the destruction of Mu or Lemuria and of the exodus from it, the origins and development of the Mayan and Incan civilization, the relationship between Egypt and Atlantis, the progress of the Egyptian civilization, and give some particulars concerning other portions of the world.[151] A couple of these are especially interesting: Cayce states that the Great Pyramid took about a century to construct and was built from 10,490 to 10,390 B.C.;[152] he also refers to the time when, in Egypt, there was the first attempt to construct a written language.[153]

From these teachings of Edgar Cayce on Atlantis, we can see the formulation for the basis of much of his readings, prophecies, medical genius, religion, doctrine, etc.

Summation of Data on Atlantis[154]

1. The Human Race has existed on earth for at least ten million years.

2. Man originated in five places, one of which was Atlantis.

3. Man originated as a non-physical entity (i.e. as a spirit); these non-physical entities entered matter and thus interrupted the evolutionary process then going on. Man in time became engrossed in material things and thus forgot his original Divine Nature and Origin.

4. Man attained great scientific knowledge and technological progress many thousands (if not longer) years ago. These equaled or excelled the current knowledge and progress.

5. Man misused his knowledge and skills; this misusage resulted in the physical disasters which overtook Atlantis (and Lemuria?).

6. During the second disaster Atlantis was divided into a group of islands; after the third, it essentially ceased to exist.

7. Strife between groups was characteristic of these periods and may have precipitated the disasters.

8. A great deal of discord existed over the entities described as "things."

NOTES

[1] *New York Times,* July 19, 1967

[2] Edgar E. Cayce, *Atlantis—Fact or Fiction?* p. 11

[3] In his more recent publication, he states that 700 individuals, out of the 1600 different persons for whom the 2500 life readings were given, had incarnations in Atlantis which influenced their present life. See Edgar Evans Cayce, *Edgar Cayce on Atlantis,* p. 27

[4] Readings 5748-1 and 5748-2. Some confusion exists as to the content of the subsections of reading 5748 between that printed in *Atlantis—Fact or Fiction?*

pp. 12-14, and that in *Edgar Cayce on Atlantis*, pp. 48f

[5] *Vid.* reading no. 5748-1

[6] It is not clear from this reading whether the Garden of Eden is equivalent to Caucasia or Carpathia or both, or perhaps neither. See reading 364-13. Elsewhere, Cayce seems to have located Eden in Atlantis

[7] Reading 364-13

[8] Reading 364-13

[9] "The civilizations of Da and Lemuria were developed thousands of years before Atlantis, and the Lemurian overlapped the Atlantean before Lemuria sank into the sea." (Eula Allen, *The River of Time*, p. 6)

[10] Reading 364-3

[11] *Vid.* Reading 364-13, cf. *Vid.* Reading 364-6

[12] Reading 5748-1; cf. also 364-13

[13] Reading no. 2665-2, dated July 17, 1925

[14] Reading 364-6

[15] Readings 5249-1; 5056-1

[16] Reading 364-11

[17] Allan, *Op. Cit.*, P. 25

[18] *Vid.*, e.g., 1406-1; 1417-1

[19] Readings no. 3022-1; 900-340

[20] Reading 364-12 (1932)

[21] Readings no. 2126-1; 1745-1; 897-26. See also 3022-1

[22] Apparently also those constituted five nations. Reading 5748-3

[23] The red race developed in Atlantis and in America

[24] *Vid.* Also 364-3 and 364-9

[25] *Vid.* Reading 364-3; and 364-9

[26] Reading no. 364-13

[27] Reading 294-149

[28] Although Dr. Carleton S. Coon of the University of Pennsylvania Museum suggests that man divided into five races about 500,000 years ago (*The Origins of the Races.* New York: Alfred Knopf, 1962)

[29] *Vid.* 5056-1. *Vid.* also 2753-2; 2121-2

[30] *Vid.* Reading 5056-1

[31] Readings 618-3; 866-1

[32] Readings 263-4; 621-1; 1315-2; 1378-1; 1416-1; 1417-1; 1474-1; 1968-2; See also 877-26

[33] Reading 1999-1

[34] *Vid.* 1292-1; 1406-1 & 1968-2

[35] Reading 364-4
[36] Reading 364-4
[37] Reading 364-11
[38] *Vid.* reading 364-3. Reading 3645 and 364-7
[39] *Vid.* 364-11
[40] *Vid.* 877-26
[41] *Vid.* 877-26
[42] *Vid.* 877-26. cf readings 2753-2; 5037-1
[43] *Vid.* Reading 5249-1
[44] *Vid.* 1968-2
[45] *Vid.* Reading 364-4. cf. Allen, *Op. Cit.*, p. 38
[46] Readings 2749-1; 2157-1; 1023-2; 1735-2. cf. 2072-10
[47] Readings 1730-1
[48] Readings 1735-2
[49] *Vid.* 2157-1 and 1730-1
[50] Readings 813-1; 1470-1; 2494-1
[51] Reading 262-39
[52] *Vid.* 621-1
[53] Reading 263-4; *Vid.* also 877-26 and 2157-1
[54] Reading 2562-1. cf. reading 2560-1
[55] e.g., *Vid.* 263-4
[56] *Vid.* 363-2
[57] *Vid.* 364-11
[58] The Garden of Eden apparently was located somewhere in Atlantis. *Vid.* readings 364-7 and 364-4. cf. reading 390-2
[59] The reading 364-11 indicates that the disaster in the area of the Sargasso Sea occurred 7,500 years before the final destruction of Atlantis. If the final disaster refers to the third destruction, then the date would be c. 17,500 B.C. or between the Second and Third disasters
[60] *Vid.* 262-39; 2749-1; 5249-1; 2157-1; cf. 2470-2; 2675-4; 2893-1; 2855-1
[61] *Vid.* e.g., 262-32
[62] *Vid.* 1378-1 and 877-26
[63] *Vid.* 364-6; 364-13; 5249-1
[64] *Vid.* e.g., 364-4
[65] *Vid.* reading 877-26
[66] Readings 2437-1; 2004-1; 1859-1 and 1574-1
[67] Reading 2494-1
[68] Readings 813-1; 2856-1; *Vid.* reading 1574-1
[69] Reading 38-1

[70] Readings 282-2; 519-1; 1003-1; 1861-2; 2122-1; 4361-1
[71] Readings 440-5; 820-1
[72] Reading 187-1
[73] Reading 2464-2
[74] Reading 234-1
[75] Reading 416-1
[76] *Vid.* 1574-1
[77] *Vid.* 38-1
[78] Reading 2124-3
[79] *Vid.* 2856-1
[80] *Vid.* 187-1
[81] *Vid.* 159-1 and 4361-1
[82] *Vid.* e.g., readings 38-1; 2464-2; and 3034-1
    cf. readings 390-2; 640-1, 1744-1 and 3479-2
[83] *Vid.* 1744-1 and 2462-2
[84] Reading 2390-1
[85] Readings 470-22; 1792-2 and 3376-2. Also readings
    640-1 and 813-1; 1744-1; and 2462-2
[86] *Vid.* reading 470-22
[87] *Vid.* readings 470-22 and 3376-2
[88] Readings 1626-1; 3034-1; 5245-1
[89] *E.G.* readings 280-1 and 3034-1
[90] *Vid.* readings 2464-2 and 5245-1. cf. also 1302-2
[91] Reading 3633-1; also 640-1
[92] Readings 3654-1; *Vid.* also 3479-2; and 2462-2
[93] *Vid.* 820-1. 1792-2; cf. readings 1298-1; 2897-1; and
    2913-1
[94] *Vid.* reading 1859-1; cf. reading 4353-4
[95] *Vid.* readings 390-2; 416-1; 640-1; 1298-1; 1626-1;
    2390-1; 3479-2; 3633-1; and 3654-1; and 5245.
    Vid. also reading 5096-1
[96] *Vid.* 812-1; 444-1; 813-1
[97] *Vid.* e.g. reading 2390-1
[98] *Vid.* readings 813-1; 497-1; 1849-2; 470-22
[99] *Vid.* e.g. reading 1298-1
[100] *Vid.* readings 390-2 and 441-1. cf. with reading 877-26
    which suggests that the division into islands resulted
    from the first not the second destruction
[101] *Vid.* reading 884-1
[102] *Vid.* reading 470-22
[103] *Vid.* readings 1298-1; 1861-2; and 5096-1
[104] *Vid.* reading 2147-1
[105] *Vid.* reading 3574-2

[106] *Vid.* reading 2147-1
[107] *Vid.* readings 445-1; 991-1; 1872-1; 2002-1
[108] *Vid.* readings 1554-1; 2163-1; 2280-1
[109] *Vid.* reading 2077-1
[110] *Vid.* readings 281-43; 1007-3; 1152-1; 1404-1; 1837-1; 2153-1; 2524-1; 5118-1; 5750-1
[111] *Vid.* reading 1152-1
[112] *Vid.* reading 3184-1
[113] *Vid.* readings 1695-1; 2144-1
[114] *Vid.* reading 440-1
[115] *Vid.* reading 914-1
[116] *Vid.* reading 1610-2
[117] *Vid.* readings 2031-1; 2077-1; 2419-1; 2153-3
[118] *Vid.* reading 1574-1
[119] Vid. reading 2677-1
[120] *Vid.* reading 1842-1
[121] *Vid.* reading 2147-1
[122] *Vid.* reading 1751-1
[123] *Vid.* reading 2002-1
[124] *Vid.* reading 2272-1
[125] *Vid.* readings 1641-1; 2524-1
[126] *Vid.* reading 2677-1
[127] *Vid.* reading 1177-1
[128] *Vid.* reading 378-13
[129] *Vid.* readings 955-1; 1082-3; *Vid.* also 1610-2
[130] *Vid.* readings 1120-1; 1033-1
[131] *Vid.* readings 1082-1; 1610-2
[132] *Vid.* reading 2483-2
[133] *Vid.* readings 1731-1; 2922-1
[134] *Vid.* reading 378-13
[135] *Vid.* readings 1143-2; 2154-1; 2763-1
[136] *Vid.* readings 774-1; 2927-1
[137] *Vid.* reading 364-6
[138] *Vid.* readings 991-1; 378-13
[139] *Vid.* reading 1744-1
[140] *Vid.* reading 339-1
[141] Acts 7:51
[142] *Vid.* readings 2147-1; 2537-1
[143] *Vid.* reading 1007-3
[144] *Vid.* reading 1007-3
[145] *Vid.* readings 708-1; 1123-1; 2283-1; 2677-1; *Vid.* also 423-3; 439-1; 797-1; 955-1; 1007-1; 1007-3; 1177-1; 1458-1; 1842-1; 2916-1; 3545-1

[146] *Vid.* readings 2283-1; 2916-1; 3541-1; 2677-1; cf. 315-4; 633-2; 1123-1

[147] *Vid.* readings 1599-1; 1710-3; 5750-1

[148] *Vid.* reading 3611-1

[149] Vid. reading 914-1

[150] *Vid.* reading 5750-1

[151] *Vid.* e.g.; readings 378-16; 470-22; 516-2; 585-10; 519-1; 559-7; 1167-2; 1472-1; 1481-1; 1681-1; 2012-1; 2402-2; 2537-1; 2916-1; 2823-2; 3575-2; 3645-1

[152] *Vid.* reading 5748-6. This event occurred about four centuries before the final disappearance of Atlantis (c. 10,000 B.C.)

[153] *Vid.* reading 516-2

[154] *Vid. Edgar Cayce on Atlantis,* pp. 82, 101

6. EDGAR CAYCE ON REINCARNATION

IT WAS through his association with Arthur Lammers that Edgar Cayce came to believe in reincarnation. It became the center of his religious philosophy, his readings, and his followers in the A.R.E. For them, no one can know or read the Bible unless it is interpreted in the light of reincarnation. This is clearly revealed by Lytle W. Robinson's story: "The Bible is like the Irishman's fence, three feet high and three feet thick. If the wind blows it over, it is still a fence. It has just been moved three feet, that's all. No damage is done, nothing is added, nothing is taken away; only its position has been changed.

"With that as a criterion, let us seek after its truth with enlightenment, for within that fence lies an esoteric meaning far more profound than meets the naked eye. Reincarnation is not new, but it opens up for the Christian Bible student a new realm of understanding."[1]

Of course, the analogy used is poor. If the wind blows the fence over, it is no longer a fence; if it was blown three feet, it is no longer on the original foundation. The same would be true of the Scriptures. One does not interpret the Bible in the light of reincarnation, without destroying some part of it. One does not subjectively approach the Bible with the intention of reading reincarnation into it without removing the Bible from its original foundation.

According to Edgar Cayce, "all souls were creat-

ed in the beginning.'" Each soul or entity enters
into the earthplane as a human being. Upon death,
the soul leaves and eventually re-enters, having
subconscious access to the characteristics, mental
capacities and skills it has accumulated in previous
lives. This subconscious access is the basis for
karma, a universal law of cause and effect which
provides the soul with opportunities of physical,
mental and spiritual growth.

Reincarnation even extended into the life of our
Lord and Saviour Jesus Christ. "First in the beginning, of course; and then as Enoch, Melchizedek,
in the perfection. Then in the earth of Joseph,
Joshua, Jeshua, Jesus.'"

In fact, the readings clearly teach that Adam was
not the first man, but merely the reincarnation of
Amilius. "In the beginning as Amilius, as Adam,
as Melchizedek, as Zend (?), as Ur (?), as Asaph
(?), as Jeshua—Joseph—Jesus.'" Now the apostle
Paul clearly contradicts this reincarnation theory
when he declared that "the first man (was) Adam.'"

Reincarnation for Edgar Cayce and the A.R.E. is
based on human reasoning. "Since we 'all have
sinned and come short of the glory of God,' (Romans
3:23), we would be doomed if we had only one life
for making ourselves acceptable to the Father.'" "If
we deny that Christ included reincarnation in the
laws He came to 'uphold but not to change,' we face
the fact that He was demanding of His followers an
almost superhuman exercise of blind faith . . . He
was offering a hit-or-miss, one-chance-only doctrine.'"

Even if we had several lifetimes "for making ourselves acceptable to the Father," we could never
make it.' God declares us to be righteous, not on
the ground of our own righteousness, but solely on

the basis of the impeccable righteousness of Jesus Christ. This is in accord with the context of Romans 3:23. "For all have sined, and come short of the glory of God." God is the One Who declares righteous all those who believe in Jesus Christ (v. 26); declaring them righteous "by his grace through the redemption that is in Christ Jesus: Whom God hath set forth to be a propitiation through faith in his blood, to declare his righteousness for the remission of sins that are past." (vv. 24, 25)

We are not "doomed if we had only one life for making ourselves acceptable to the Father,"[9] for in this one life, God is ready to forgive our sins and declare us righteous through faith in Jesus Christ. It is not "hit or miss," for the Bible tells us that "as many as received him, to them gave he the authority to become the children of God."[10] But there remains only One in whom we can stand acceptable to the Father, and that is Jesus Christ.[11]

There is no room for reincarnation nor a need for it when one reads the Bible and discovers the answer to life in Jesus Christ. Let us never forget the marvelous prayer of David in Psalm 17:14-15. "From men which are thy hand, O Lord, from men of the world, which have their portion in this life, and whose belly thou fillest with thy hidden treasure: they are full of children, and leave the rest of their substance to their babes. *As for me, I will behold thy face IN RIGHTEOUSNESS: I shall be satisfied, WHEN I AWAKE, WITH THY LIKENESS.*"

NOTES

[1] Robinson, Lytle W. "Reincarnation and the Scriptures," *The Searchlight*. Oct. 15, 1952. Vol. IV, No. 25, p. 1
[2] Reading 5749-3
[3] Reading 5749-14
[4] Reading 364-7
[5] I Corinthians 15:45
[6] Robinson, Lytle W., *Op. Cit.*, p. 4
[7] *The Hidden History of Reincarnation*, p. 42
[8] Ephesians 2:8, 9; Titus 3:5
[9] Robinson, Lytle W., *Op. Cit.*, p. 4
[10] John 1:12
[11] Acts 4:12, John 14:6, I Timothy 2:5

7. EDGAR CAYCE AND CHRISTIAN DOCTRINE

In the following doctrines, the teachings of Edgar Cayce as presented in his readings are stated along with the teaching of Scripture on a given doctrine.

It should be noted that the Bible is God's special revelation to man, setting forth objectively what God would have us to know about man and his world, and about Himself, in a perspicuous and self-interpreting manner. If the source of Edgar Cayce's readings is God, then one would expect Scripture and the readings to be non-contradictory. However, when one applies the same hermeneutical principle (i.e. a literal interpretation—what the text says at face value) to both Scripture and Cayce's Readings, one discovers a good number of contradictions. Since Scripture is God's revelation, and God cannot contradict Himself, the contradictions therefore lie in the readings of Edgar Cayce.

God

"There are three things that are abominable in the eyes of that *creative force* from which all good emanates: Pride of the eye, pride of the heart, and deceitfulness of the lust of the flesh.'"

In the readings of Edgar Cayce and the A.R.E., God is presented as an impersonal force, often referred to in the readings as the "creative force" or "universal creative energy."

The Bible very clearly teaches us in numerous references that God is a Personal Being—a Personal God, to whom the pronouns "I," "Thou," and "He" can be meaningfully applied. He performs acts that only a personality is capable of: God knows (II Tim. 2:19); God has a will (I John 2:17); God sees (Gen. 1:4); God hears (Exodus 2:24); etc. The God which the Bible declares is an all-powerful, all-knowing, all-seeing everywhere present Personality. He most certainly is not the God proclaimed by Edgar Cayce and the A.R.E., for they speak of a "creative force" or "creative energy," and "it" does not have a personality, nor can "it" be addressed as a Personal being.

Trinity

"What is the Godhead?"

"Father, Son and Holy Spirit. There is an outpouring of the spirit on thee as ye pour it out upon thy fellow-man. For, as ye do it unto the least of thy brethren, ye do it unto thy Maker. For, until ye have seen in the purpose of each soul—though in error he may be, that ye would worship in thy Maker, ye have not begun to think straight. For, God is one Lord, one law, that abideth aright in the hearts of those who seek to do and to know His biddings. Then, empty self—as ye did of old—of self. For ye must come before the throne empty-handed if ye would have thy hands, thy heart, thy mind filled with the goodness of the Lord.

"Then as thy body, thy mind, and thy soul are but the three-dimensional phases of the concept of the Godhead, use each as such.

"For as ye perceive, ye are in a three-dimensional consciousness of the earth; yet in Jupiter, Mercury, Venus, Uranus, ye may be in the four, five, seven, eight. These are a part, then, of the eternal turmoil, as one perceives in the three-dimensional consciousness. They manifest in the three-dimensional Godhead. Father, Son and Holy Spirit. They are one even as thy body, thy mind and thy soul are one."[2]

It is indeed humorous to note in this reading that we perceive God as triune because we live in a three-dimensional planet. If God is the God of the universe, which the readings admit, then He either exists as three Persons in the entire universe, or He does not.

In Matthew 3:16-17 and Matthew 28:19 it is very clear that three distinct Persons are viewed as the one God. Even in the Old Testament, the Unity of God is declared: "The Lord our God is one Lord." (Deuteronomy 6:4). Yet, in Genesis 1:26 and 11:7, God is referred to as plural, a plural unity. In the New Testament, God is still one God (Galatians 3:20). Yet Jesus is God (John 1:1-3; John 8:58); the Holy Spirit is God (Acts 5:3-4); and the Father is God (Galatians 1:1).

Therefore God is declared as three distinct Persons, the Father, the Son, and the Holy Spirit; and He is one God.

This is certainly not the position of the A.R.E. and the readings of Edgar Cayce. They deny the Triune God of Christianity and the Bible.

Hell

"That as builded by self; as those emblematical influences are shown through the experiences of the beloved in that builded, that created. For, each soul is a portion of creation—and builds that in a portion of its experience that is, through its physical mental or spiritual mental, has builded for itself. And each entity's heaven or hell must, through some experience be that which it has builded for itself. Is thy hell one that is filled with fire or brimstone? But no, each and every soul is tried so as by fire, purified, purged; for he, though he were the Son, learned obedience through the things which he suffered.'"

Heaven and Hell are not experiences or temporary states we pass through in this lifetime. The Bible clearly teaches eternal conscious punishment and torment for those who reject Jesus Christ as Lord and Saviour. They will remain in future everlasting torment, separated from the presence of the Lord (I Thessalonians 1:9). For Biblical evidence that real torment and everlasting conscious separation from God exist see Matthew 13:42, 5; Luke 13:24-28; 16:19-31; II Peter 2:17; Jude 13; Revelation 14:11-11; Revelation 19:20; 20:10, etc.

Edgar Cayce may speak of hell as a present state of experience, but the Bible declares hell to be the present and future habitation for those who have died without accepting Jesus Christ as Lord and Saviour.

The Bible

"One of the most important concepts in the readings, I believe, is the threefold meaning of the Bible for you and me.

"First, the people actually lived. Abraham was a living, breathing individual. . .

"Second, each character in the Bible symbolizes

faith. He was called father of the faithful. Jesus gave the example . . . Abraham's bosom—a state of consciousness, a place of attainment in the beggar's development which could best be described as Abraham's bosom—a symbol for the place of rest for all who are faithful.

"Third, these symbols are applicable to us today. At various times in our lives, we can all be an Abraham and step forward with faith.'"

The first point presents no problem to the Biblical student, but the second point does. "Each character in the Bible symbolizes faith." When the Bible interprets a symbol, we are on safe ground. Otherwise, care should be exercised. One must heartily urge that each character in the Bible does not symbolize faith. Satan and his followers do not symbolize the type of faith a follower of Jesus Christ should have. Nowhere in Scripture is there a statement that interprets every character in the Bible as a symbol of faith.

The third point, that "these symbols are applicable to us today," is not true when viewed in the A.R.E. perspective. The Bible is applicable to our lives today in proclaiming God's Love in the Person of Jesus Christ, Whom God sent into the world to be the satisfaction for our sins (I John 4:8-10). It is the Bible that is able to make us "wise unto salavation through faith which is in Christ Jesus" (II Timothy 3:15).

It is the Bible which "is profitable for doctrine, for reproof, for correction, for instruction in righteousness; that the man of God may be perfect, thoroughly furnished unto all good works." (II Timothy 3:16-17).

This is entirely different from the view of the A.R.E. and Edgar Cayce, who would have us believe the Bible to be full of symbols, which one must interpret in the light of the readings given by Edgar Cayce. They have reduced the Word of God written to the Word of God symbolic, God's revelation to mankind to Edgar Cayce's revelation of God to mankind.

Church

"The essential principles of the great religions, the readings insisted, were nevertheless, all the same. They were only clothed in different garments."" "Study the truths of the oneness of all faiths in God's force. For they are one; whether Jewish, Gentile, Greek or heathen."" The readings of Edgar Cayce at the A.R.E. declare their mystical movement and religion to be essentially syncretistic. People from all religions and faiths seem to be able to reconcile their faith with the metaphysical philosophy emerging from these readings.

The Bible tells us that there is the Church Mystical, that which contains all those who have been born again through the Spirit of God; and that there is also the Church Institutional, the public assembling of believers for fellowship with God and with one another.

In the New Testament the Church is spoken of as "the church of God," "the Churches in Christ," "the Churches of God . . . in Christ Jesus." It is clearly noticed that the significant feature of the Church in her relationship to God and to Jesus Christ.

Despite the syncretistic cries of the A.R.E. and the readings of Edgar Cayce that "the essential principles of the great religions . . . were nevertheless, all the same," the Church is founded upon

Jesus Christ, and salvation comes only by faith in Jesus Christ as Lord and Saviour. (Acts 4:12). No one can come to the Father, unless they come through Jesus Christ (John 14:6). Jesus Christ is the only way, the only one whereby "we must be saved" (Acts 4:12).

Salvation

"Through the guidance of the Christ-soul the earth has been made a ladder up which souls may return to a consciousness of atonement with the creator."[7]

"Until there is redemption through the acceptance of the law, or love of God, as manifested through the Channel or the Way, there can be little or no development in a material or spiritual plane."[8]

Their concept of Salvation is that our souls, often referred to as entities, must experience atonement with God. We may have to re-enter the material world many times before we achieve this. This position is more commonly known as reincarnation, which is undoubtedly the position of the A.R.E. This teaching is contrary to many of the concepts structured by and in the Bible, particularly those regarding Sin, Redemption, Eternal Life and Eternal Separation from God, etc. Rather than accept the "vicarious" or substitutionary atonement of Jesus Christ on Calvary's Cross, they have substituted "Karma," a chain of cause and effect, whereby every soul has its own Karma which it inherits from the past, and continues to create in Karma by its action in the present. It is basically a system of continuous good works—past, present, and future.

This is not God's revealed plan for the perfection of the soul (Ephesians 2:8, 9; Galatians 2:16). It is only through faith in the Lord Jesus Christ (and His completed work at Calvary for our sins) that anyone will ever be declared righteous before God and be given eternal life.

The Bible clearly teaches us that following death, the soul does not pass through a series of future reincarnations. If you accept Jesus Christ as your Lord and Saviour, your soul will, at death, enter into the presence of the Lord (Philippians 1:23). If you reject Him, your soul will, at death, enter into a place of conscious, eternal separation from the Lord (II Peter 2:9). But in either case, reincarnation is not God's revealed plan for the perfecting of the soul. "And as it is appointed unto men once to die, but after this the judgment" (Hebrews 9:27). Reincarnation finds no place in a theology which says "Ye *are* complete in Him" (Colossians 2:10). The two views are mutually exclusive.

So we can see that Edgar Cayce and the A.R.E. reject a personal and Triune God, Hell as a place of eternal conscious torment, the Bible as the Word of God written, The Church as the mystical body of believers in Jesus Christ, apart from whom there is no salvation, and salvation as a gift of God, apart from works, "lest any man should boast" (Ephesians 2:8, 9). This then is the devilish system devised to detour people around Calvary's Cross and the one who died upon it for our sins.

NOTES

1. Reading 254-34
2. Reading 3188-1
3. Reading 281-16
4. Turner, Gladys Davis, "The Bible and You," *The Searchlight,* Vol. IX, May 1957, No. 5, p. 3
5. Robinson, Lytle W., *Edgar Cayce,* p. 3
6. *Edgar Cayce*
7. *Venture Inward,* p. 64
8. *Ibid.,* p. 122

8. EDGAR CAYCE AND JESUS CHRIST

WHEN IT comes to Christology, the doctrine of
the Person and Work of our Lord and Saviour
Jesus Christ, the heresies of Edgar Cayce are very
clear.

According to the readings, "Christ is not a man.
Jesus was the man. Christ was the messenger . . .
Christ in all ages. Jesus only in one.'"

*The Bible nowhere declares such a distinction
between Jesus and Christ.* One can quite clearly
note in the Bible references to Christ as a man (I
Corinthians 15:21, 22) and to "the blood of
Christ" (Ephesians 2:13) which requires Him to
be a man. Jesus Christ is the God-man, second
Person of the Trinity. The Bible says *"Jesus
Christ,* the same yesterday, and today and forever"
(Hebrews 13:8). Nowhere does the Bible declare
the Lord from Heaven to be Jesus "indwelt by the
Christ" but rather Scripture dogmatically declares
Him to be "God manifest in the flesh" (I Timothy
3:16). Moreover, the apostle John specifically iden-
tifies the Incarnation as including both appella-
tions Jesus and Christ (I John 4:2, 8). Furthermore, using the present tense, John identifies
Jesus as the Christ. And the aged apostle penned
these lines many decades after the Crucifixion.

Incarnation

"Please list the names of the incarnation of the
Christ, and of Jesus, indicating where the develop-

ment of the man Jesus began."² "First in the beginning, of course; and then as Enoch, Melchizedek, in the perfection. Then in the earth of Joseph, Joshua, Jeshua, Jesus."³

One cannot accept reincarnation as a substitute for the incarnation of Jesus Christ. Truly the Incarnation was miraculous and unique. That which was conceived by the Holy Spirit was "God manifest in the flesh" (I Timothy 3:16). One would affirm that He, in whom there was no sin, is eternally unchangeable⁴—in the light of which the suppositions of reincarnation are seen as farcical. *Perfection needs no improvement.* Moreover, His righteousness is reckoned ours in the atonement.

Sinlessness of Christ

"When did the knowledge come to Jesus that He was to be the Saviour of the World?"

"When He fell, in Eden."⁵

Edgar Cayce and the A.R.E. proclaim Jesus to have sinned, but it was our Lord indeed who challenged His enemies to convince Him of sin.⁶ Before He was born, the angel declared Him to be "holy," without sin.⁷ It was because He was without sin, "who knew no sin," that He could be our substitute on the cross, take our place, and become "sin for us," "that we might be made the righteousness of God in him."⁸ It was Christ who "was in all points tempted like as we are, yet without sin."⁹

The Atonement of Jesus Christ

"The fulfilling of 'without the shedding of blood there is no remission of sin.' Hence His blood was shed as the sacrifice of the just for the unjust, that all may stand in the same light with the Father."[10]

This is clearly universal salvation. Jesus died "that *all* may stand in the same light with the Father." The sacrifice of Jesus Christ on Calvary's cross is sufficient to provide salvation for all. But God has declared in the Bible that many will not accept His provision of redemption; and therefore the sacrifice of His Son will condemn to eternal torment and separation from God those who reject it. Those who teach that the atonement is provided for all men, and that God is a God of love, must bear in mind the consequence for all who reject His love in the Person of His Son, Jesus Christ, who died for us.

Resurrection of Jesus Christ

"Then, as the body of Christ and the flesh became perfect in the world, as it was laid aside on the cross and in the tomb, the physical body moved away—through what man come to know as dimension—and the spirit was then able to take hold of that being in the way in which it entered again into the body. Thus, it presents itself to the world, as it did to individuals at the time and as it does to man (in general) at present."[11]

This concept of the Resurrection of Jesus Christ is nothing more than His Reincarnation in another body. According to the readings, the Christ appeared in Enoch and in Melchizedek before it was reincarnated in Jesus.

But one need only read the fifteenth chapter of Corinthians, where the doctrine of the physical resurrection of the body to immortality is clearly stated, answering the argument of reincarnation vs resurrection.

In John 20:25-28, Thomas doubted the literal physical resurrection of Christ, only to urgently repent after Jesus presented His body for examination. It was the same one that was crucified, bearing the nail prints and the spear wound. Despite the readings of Edgar Cayce at the A.R.E., no reasonable person will say that the body displayed by Jesus to Thomas was not His crucifixion body. This is particularly validated by the text of John 2:18-22. Jesus Christ there specifically identified the resurrection body with the one He then occupied—months before His death.

"In one Reading an individual asked if he could gain perfection in this lifetime. (So as not to have to return to earth again.) The sleeping Cayce flippantly replied, 'Why should you expect to do in one lifetime what it took the Master thirty lives to attain?' "[12]

Edgar Cayce's definition of resurrection as reincarnation,[13] his statement that Christ needed thirty lives to attain perfection,[14] and his belief that Christ was resurrected[15] pose a great problem. One might ask if Christ attained perfection after thirty lives, why did He need to be reincarnated (which is Cayce's definition of resurrection)? It is quite clear that the two terms, resurrection and reincarnation, are not synonomous.

Thus we can see in Edgar Cayce and the A.R.E. a denial of Person and Work of Jesus Christ; for they deny that Jesus Christ is "God manifest in the flesh," the sinlessness of His life on earth, the sufficiency of His atonement on Calvary's Cross, and His bodily resurrection from the dead. The "Jesus Christ" of Edgar Cayce and the A.R.E. is not the Jesus Christ of the Bible and History. Truly the warning of Paul to the Corinthians of those "false apostles, deceitful workers" who preach "another Jesus," "another spirit" and "another gospel"[16] is valid today in the teachings of the late Edgar Cayce and the A.R.E.

NOTES

[1] Reading 991-1
[2] Reading 5749-14
[3] *Ibid.*
[4] I John 3:5; Hebrews 4:15; 13:8
[5] Reading 2067-7
[6] John 8:46
[7] Luke 1:35
[8] II Corinthians 5:21
[9] Hebrews 4:15
[10] Reading 5749-10
[11] Reading 8337-168
[12] Furst, Jeffrey, *Edgar Cayce's Story of Jesus,* New York: Coward-McCann: 1969, page 71
[13] Reading 5749-8
[14] Furst, Jeffery, *Op. Cit.,* page 71
[15] Readings 5749-10; 295-993; 1158; etc.
[16] II Corinthians 11:4

BOOK REVIEWS

MILLARD, JOSEPH: *Edgar Cayce/Mystery Man of MIRACLES*. The Edgar Cayce Foundation, Inc., 1967. 224 pp.

Approached from a purely literary perspective, this biography of the famous "Sleeping Prophet" might be categorized as workman-like, and little more. However, the cumulative impact of the fantastic events recorded therein transcends the mechanics of the presentation, leading this reviewer to conclude that the story rescues the book. For the life of Edgar Cayce was *different*, to say the least—a classic in itself, presenting the writer with a glorious opportunity to produce something of literary significance: He has not.

Cayce, when in his famous trances, dealt with phenomenal prognostic accuracy concerning people and situations of whom and of which he was totally ignorant when conscious. Thus he produced medical cures, etc., of a breathtaking nature.

A person of evidently vast psychic propensity, his astonishing career must evoke debate in at least two areas of consideration: (1) the question of the analysis and consequent validity of the phenomena; and (2) the source(s) of said phenomena. Scientists and sleuths will discuss the former—theologians will argue the latter. It is perhaps most significant that, despite a strong Bible atmosphere, this biography produces little evidence in Cayce's life that would either Christologically or soteriologically sit well in the courts of historic Christianity.

The sympathetic involvement with reincarnation and astrology are demonstrably contrary to the structure of Biblical religion. One wonders, moreover, at the "reading" that suggested visiting a modern-day protagonist of the ancient Gnostic heresy . . . Certainly, as a person immersed in Scriptural lore, Cayce was nonetheless a relatively easy mark for cultic mysticism.

Morally, this book presents Edgar Cayce as a man of most commendable virtue—one who, for instance, opposed remuneration for his unusual services throughout a great portion of his life. It took a long while before he was persuaded otherwise (a triumph, this reviewer believes, for practicality!) . . . An evidently gentle and ethical man, Cayce exhibited much of the demeanor one would be pleased to call Christ-like: This, Millard's account clearly demonstrates.

Yet, the inquirer's thinking must repeatedly return to the nagging question concerning the *source* of the phenomena. Evidently psychic and clairvoyant, his career produced much data that must interest the student of demonology. Among other things, one notes that his "trance" voice would refer to itself in the first person plural; also, the voice bore phraseological evidences difficult to assign to a heavenly origin. The occurrence of fires likewise presents an intriguing area of inquiry.

As an incidental consideration, the author's prolific use of direct quotes throughout seemingly inaccessible parts of Cayce's history, together with the lack of psychic *failures* found in this book— these are factors which I believe merit criticism: At such instances, objectivity perches on the window-ledge.

Edgar Cayce appears to have been an altruistic benefactor whose trance-oriented words ministered graciously to the temporal needs of society. His amazing and humanitarian life makes this book recommended reading. Orthodox Christianity must, however, sadly reflect on such anomalies as "Biblical" astrology and reincarnation. The Christian soteriology allows for none of this.

In 1945, at the age of 68, Edgar Cayce died.

Cayce, Hugh Lynn: *VENTURE INWARD*. New York: Harper & Row, 1964. 227 pp.

The book, *VENTURE INWARD*, was written by Hugh Lynn Cayce, the son of the late Edgar Cayce. Before discussing the book as such, a little bit of information about the author is probably pertinent. As compared to others, Hugh Lynn Cayce does not seem to be nearly as dogmatic in his statements. Rather, he seems to be one who, at least at first, has had great difficulty in accepting many of the ideas which came forth in Edgar Cayce's readings. Perhaps this is part of the reason why, although he seems to accept many of these ideas now, his approach is still one of asking questions and looking for more information, rather than in making dogmatic statements.

VENTURE INWARD differs from many of the other books which are written about Edgar Cayce in that it is not only a biography. The first section of the book is a biography and occupies approximately 78 pages out of the book. This biography is of great value to the researcher and to the interested public because it is written from the perspective of

the subject's son, and therefore, has many pieces of
information in it which are not only descriptive of
the subject but of his actual relationship with the
author. It is interesting to trace through the biographical section the author's reactions to the un-
folding drama in his father's life. Besides the basic
biographical sketch, he deals with his life in terms
of the expanding abilities of his subconscious mind
in two sections entitled: "A HELPFUL UNCON-
SCIOUSNESS" and "A BOUNDLESS UNCON-
SCIOUS." This is in keeping with Mr. Cayce's basic attitude towards his father's abilities as well as
toward the many different types of phenomena and
experiences discussed in the latter sections of the
book. His basic position seems to be that most of
these phenomena come from the resources and hidden depths of the unconscious, or at least from the
direction of the unconscious with other areas of existence. This basic theory, or approach to the subject, is the basis for the latter sections of the
book. The second section, entitled "TWO TRADI-
TIONAL AND SOMETIMES PROFESSIONAL
DOORWAYS TO THE UNCONSCIOUS," con-
sists of two chapters in which Mr. Cayce discusses
hypnosis and mediumship. He discusses the hypnosis, giving a rather interesting and historical background in terms of the Cayce readings, especially
in terms of the idea of a person's "aura," and in
connection with other supposed life forces and cur-
rents which are found in the human body. Again,
it should be stated that he does not say that certain
things are definitely true; rather, he suggests possibilities and asks questions in connection with the
scientific facts as we have them in comparison with
the Cayce readings. In the sixth chapter of this
section on mediumship, he discusses spiritualism

from the same basic type of perspective. The next section, entitled "DANGEROUS DOORWAYS TO THE UNCONSCIOUS," applies some of the same principles or approaches to such areas as automatic writing and ouija boards, ESP and mental cases, possession by other spirits, dianetics, and scientology, as well as the subject of peyote, mushrooms, and LSD. He considers these approaches as being dangerous and does not recommend them. It is the experience of this reviewer to have known Christians who have tried to fool with ouija boards in a sense of a game and have soon found out that it was not necessarily games that were occurring and had to quickly drop the use of these things, seeing that they became potential sources of Satan or other unclean or demonic spirits to influence their lives.

The last section is entitled "SAFER DOORWAYS TO THE UNCONSCIOUS" and dealing with such subjects as dreams, telepathy, etc. It concludes with a number of sections on meditation and the activities of the A.R.E.; one of the sections being entitled "THE PLACE OF THE SMALL GROUP IN THE SPIRITUAL SEARCH," a discussion of how A.R.E. study groups operate.

One of the very valuable features of this book is the extensive bibliography found at the end of each chapter. It is especially helpful in that it consists not only of books, but also such things as newspaper articles, radio programs, magazine articles, readings on reincarnation, and books with only sections on Edgar Cayce.

Langley, Noel: *EDGAR CAYCE ON REINCARNATION.* New York: Paperback Library, Inc., 1967. Under the editorship of Hugh Lynn Cayce. 288 pp.

The theory of reincarnation has much that appears to commend it: It produces intriguing solutions for many profound problems. But, ultimately, commendation must be as short-lived as the crumbling plausibility that stimulated it. For the failure of reincarnation lies in part within the questions it creates and fails to answer.

Edgar Cayce, the famous "sleeping prophet" of Virginia Beach, was assuredly a leading figure among historic reincarnationists. In this apologetic erected around his life's ministry, author Noel Langley (and editor Hugh Lynn Cayce) wrestle vigorously with the aforementioned difficulties, crippled in their task by an insurmountable factor: "The 'sleeping' Edgar Cayce was . . . a devoted proponent of Bible lore." (*Edgar Cayce on Reincarnation;* Pg. 7.) Cayce had read the Bible many times; yet after being staggered by reincarnation (and one Arthur Lammers), he became a convert to the reconciliation of the irreconcilable: Biblical doctrine and the concept of migratory souls. The *two are mutually exclusive.*

For one thing, history witnesses to only one sinless human being. Thus, reincarnation is branded a failure—at least for the past 35,000 years or so. Ultimately, sin must logically require a sinless vehicle of atonement. And once such an immolation is established, the need for reincarnation is obliterated. This is precisely the impact Scripture exerts against the central thesis of this book.

Author and editor have earnestly endeavoured to establish the position that a series of dark practices has adulterated and/or obscured Biblical doctrine. (Byzantine potentates Justinian and Theodora receive some heavy shelling in this area.) We are told that "Our orthodox versions of the Old and New Testaments date no further back than the sixth century . . ." (*Ibid.*, Pg. 179.) Yet there is an abundance of New Testament manuscript material dating considerably earlier than the sixth century. And what Old Testament data may lack in antiquity, it more than accomplishes in accuracy which may even surpass that of the New Testament. The fact is, both segments of the Judaeo-Christian Bible have been competently estimated at *well* over 90% in fidelity to the vanished original autographs. Langley and Cayce are most unconvincing in this area—in fact, the whole Caycian position evidences a lamentable dearth of comprehension re the Holy Book.

Some interpretations are astonishing. For instance: ". . . Jesus himself had declared that there was a spark of the divine in every human soul." (*Ibid.*, p. 183.) Moreover, as indicated in the above paragraph, there are some astonishing approaches to history as well. On page 164, Voltaire is quoted as saying: "None of the early Fathers of the Church cited a single passage from the four gospels as we accept them today."

This fantastic allegation recalls the following passage:

Many years ago, says Thomas Cooper, a party of scholarly men met at a dinner-party. During the conversation, someone in the party put a question which no one present was able to answer. The question was this:

Suppose that the New Testament had been destroyed, and every copy of it lost by the end of the third century, could it have been collected together again from the writings of the Fathers of the second and third centuries?

The question startled the company; but all were

silent. Two months afterwards one of the company called upon Sir David Dalrymple, who had been present at the dinner. Pointing to a table covered with books, Sir David said: "Look at those books. You remember the question about the New Testament and the Fathers? That question roused my curiosity, and as I possessed all the existing works of the Fathers of the second and third centuries, I commenced to search, and up to this time I have found the entire New Testament, except *eleven verses*."

Leach, Charles: *Our Bible/How We Got It.* Moody Press; Copyright 1898 by Fleming H. Revell Company; Pgs. 35-36.

Edgar Cayce on Reincarnation speaks in many areas: the man himself, individual cases, the theory of reincarnation, church history, the A.R.E., Christian theology, and Scripture—among others. In my judgment, it is irremediably hung up on the last two. And recent information suggests it may also be impaled on the subject of Atlantis.

One must observe that events—whether malignant or benign—stem from either Divine, demonic, or natural sources. The record indicates Edgar Cayce administered a benevolent gift. But, as we hear a familiar echo from an ancient page ("Skin for skin, yea, all that a man hath will he give for his life."—Job 2:4), we try to evaluate the career of this unusually-gifted man. A man whose life was lived under the shadow of Holy Scripture. And our conclusion causes us to reflect sadly upon a passage appearing on page eleven of the book we have been discussing here:

His first fear was that his subconscious faculties had suddenly been commandeered by the forces of evil, making him their unwitting tool; and he had always vowed that if ever his clairvoyant powers were to play him false, he would permit no further use of them.

Although this was in reference to Cayce's early reaction toward reincarnation, this reviewer's feeling is that the seer's apprehensiveness might well have been constructively applied to his entire career.

Thomas Sugrue: *THERE IS A RIVER/The Story of Edgar Cayce.* Published by DELL PUBLISHING CO., INC., 750 Third Avenue, New York 17, N.Y. 384 pp.

This is one of the primary works dealing with the truly remarkable career of Edgar Cayce. In recent months, mounting interest in the famous Sleeping Prophet has been amply evidenced by a tide of books about his life and the content of his "readings." Sugrue, an accomplished professional, tells the story in an interesting narrative style. He experienced the healing ministry of Cayce firsthand, and thus speaks from the vantage point of personal involvement.

In the pages of *There Is A River*, we again face the benign and humble personality of Edgar Cayce —a man of great integrity, whose driving impulse to help others characterized his life. His intensive Biblical background set the stage for a career in which clairvoyance led to proclaiming the validity of reincarnation. This latter was brought into the spotlight for Cayce by Arthur Lammers, a printer from Dayton, Ohio.

Sugrue has written of the victories and defeats with compassion and humor. The early meeting with evangelist Dwight L. Moody provides an especial point of interest.

The judgment this reviewer has felt compelled to make before, relative to Cayce, must still stand: For a person so deeply grounded in the Bible to accept the premise of reincarnation requires, it seems to me, a singular misappropriation of the basic import of the Judaeo-Christian Scriptures. New Testament passages suffer contortion when they are driven into the context of reincarnation. Christ was certainly *not* setting forth such a concept when He spoke at night with Nicodemus.

However, considered apart from his thinking on reincarnation, it is difficult to evaluate Cayce's theological position in the light of historic orthodox Christianity. God alone is eternally the final Judge. Certainly, the Bible never conceives of a progression from life to life to life, etc.: The Atonement of Christ achieves positional and then actual completion for the believer, on a once-for-all-time basis.

Edgar Cayce was a man this reviewer wishes he'd had the opportunity to meet. I hope that one day such an occasion might transpire. But, according to the Bible in which Cayce was so well versed, it must happen at the feet of the Lord Jesus Christ, by virtue of His accomplishment at Calvary's darkened hill. Upon a Biblical basis, I must still identify reincarnation with a source other than my Lord Jehovah. A non-Jehovistic source, I might add, entirely capable of doing much that is beneficial—in this life.

Furst, Jeffrey, EDGAR CAYCE'S STORY OF JESUS, New York: Coward-McCann, Inc.: 1969, 365 pages, $5.95

The title of this book is somewhat of a misnomer as this book does not deal essentially with Jesus, but rather presents the lives and works of Christ throughout His many incarnations of which Jesus was only the last.

This history of Christ is traced from Atlantis to Egypt to the Persian Empire to the Essenes and finally to Palestine. Many fantastic details are given regarding the early life of Jesus, unrecorded anywhere else in history. From age 12-16 he was taught prophecy and astrology by Judy, went to Persia, India and finally Egypt where he became an initiate in the pyramid.

The author of this book notes: "The paradox exists in the fact that much of the information which came through the sleeping Cayce was extremely alien to the awakened Edgar Cayce's manner of thinking—and especially contrary to his fundamentalist Christian background" (page 10).

The author also asks a very important question: "Was Edgar Cayce as correct about Jesus as he was about so many other things?" (page 10). Undoubtedly the historical documents which we have regarding the Person and Work of Jesus Christ clearly contradict the Readings of Edgar Cayce in numerous places. The answer to this question is that a man can be correct about many things, and yet have a distorted view and understanding of who Jesus Christ is. It happens every day.

APPENDIX

What does the future hold?

Jeane Dixon has predicted many startling events for the future. She predicts that Ethel Kennedy will remarry.[1] She believes that the marriage of Greek King Constantine and Queen Anne-Marie is presently in trouble and will climax in a separation.[2]

She has continually stated that President Richard Nixon is our last hope in solving our problems. She predicts the appointment of five new Supreme Court Justices during his term of office.[3]

She predicts that the present Government of Great Britain is destined for trouble. Many changes will occur. She also predicts that a prominent figure in England will die.[4]

Cuban dictator Fidel Castro will die but this will not be the end of Communism in Cuba.[5]

Within the next fifteen years personal income taxes will become an overpowering burden. Everything one owns will be taxed.[6]

Within the next twenty years, the Roman Catholic Church will become so divided both in doctrine and principle, it will result in a split.[7] Before the twentieth century ends, one Pope will suffer bodily harm, one will be assassinated. The power of Cardinals will rise.[8]

In 1970, the U.S.S.R. will gain undisputed power of both the sea and the airways.[9] Jeane Dixon sees Senator Ted Kennedy a bit too premature for the

Presidency in 1972.[10] There will be a woman President in the 1980's.[11] In the mid 1980's, a comet will land in a great ocean causing earthquakes and tidal waves. Jeane Dixon knows approximate landing location and will reveal it later.[12]

In the year 2000, Chinese and Mongol troops will invade the Middle East.[13] In the years 2020-30, a new Oriental faith will make a profound impact on the Christian world.[14] In the year 2025, Red China will become the "Great Conqueror." It will go to war from 2025-2037.[15] In the 2030's, one who is a great peacemaker will suddenly become a war lord. He will have great military power and will fight against Red China.[16]

Many people, including students of Biblical Prophecy, will want to know how the above predictions will relate to Jeane Dixon's future world leader (Antichrist) whose "power 'will grow mightily' until 1999, when there will be 'peace on earth to all men of good will.' "[17]

NOTES

[1] Dixon, Jeane, and Noorbergen, Rene: *My Life And Prophecies*, page 154
[2] *Ibid.*, page 155
[3] *Ibid.*, pages 143-4
[4] *Ibid.*, pages 147-8
[5] *Ibid.*, pages 141-2
[6] *Ibid.*, page 153
[7] *Ibid.*, page 143
[8] *Ibid.*, pages 156-7
[9] *Ibid.*, pages 146-7
[10] *Ibid.*, page 147
[11] *Ibid.*, pages 253-4
[12] *Ibid.*, page 142
[13] *Ibid.*, page 151

[14] *Ibid.*, pages 152-3
[15] *Ibid.*, page 157
[16] *Ibid.*, pages 140-1
[17] Montgomery, Ruth, *A Gift of Prophecy*, page 193